Thomas Rees

Miscellaneous Papers on Subjects Relating to Wales

Thomas Rees

Miscellaneous Papers on Subjects Relating to Wales

ISBN/EAN: 9783337328009

Printed in Europe, USA, Canada, Australia, Japan

Cover: Foto ©ninafisch / pixelio.de

More available books at **www.hansebooks.com**

MISCELLANEOUS PAPᴸ

ON

SUBJECTS RELATING TO WALES.

BY

THOMAS REES, D.D.

LONDON:

JOHN SNOW & Co., 2, IVY LANE, PATERNOSTᴇʀ₁

SWANSEA : E. GRIFFITHS, 11, HIGH-STREET.

1867.

TO

H. O. WILLS, ESQUIRE,

OF PARK HOUSE, COTHAM, BRISTOL,

A CHRISTIAN GENTLEMAN OF EXEMPLARY LIBERALITY,

PUBLIC SPIRIT, AND DEVOTEDNESS,

AND A MUNIFICENT SUPPORTER OF VARIOUS SCHEMES

FOR THE PROMOTION OF RELIGION AND EDUCATION IN WALES,

This Work

IS MOST RESPECTFULLY AND AFFECTIONATELY

DEDICATED,

BY HIS SINCERE AND OBLIGED FRIEND,

THE AUTHOR;

PREFACE.

Most of the Papers in this collection have appeared at different times, within the last fifteen years, in the Metropolitan or local Newspapers. The attention which some of them attracted when delivered as lectures or read at public meetings, and the constant applications for copies of the papers containing them, or information on the subjects of which they treat, which the author receives from friends who feel an interest in Wales and its affairs, have induced him to publish them in this collected form.

Wales, commercially, politically, and religiously, is becoming more important year after year. In the beginning of the present century it was only an insignificant and comparatively unknown corner of Great Britain. Since then its population has more than doubled, and its manufactories and trade have more than quintupled; and as its exhaustless resources are as yet only beginning to be developed, no one need be endowed with the gift of prophecy to see that a future of unparalleled greatness is in reserve for it. Correct information concerning such a country and its people cannot fail to be highly interesting and useful to the public. Several works on Wales and the Welsh people are already accessible to English readers, such as "The character of the Welsh as a nation," by the Rev. W. Jones, Vicar of Nevin; "Wales," by Sir Thomas Phillips; "Facts, Figures, and Statements," and the "Dissent and Morality of Wales," by the late Rev. Evan Jones (Ieuan Gwynedd); "History of Nonconformity in Wales," by the author of these papers; and last, but not least, the admirably written, comprehensive, and telling letters of the Rev. Henry Richard, on "The Social and Political condition of Wales."

As all these works, with the exception of Mr. Richard's letters, are either large and expensive, or scarce, the publication of these papers may not be deemed superfluous, and more especially as they will be found to contain statements of several interesting facts not referred to in any of the fore-named works.

Were an apology necessary for the multiplication of works in the English language on Wales and its inhabitants, it might be found in the glaring ignorance which educated Englishmen, even editors of newspapers, popular authors, and prominent members of Parliament, too often betray when writing or speaking on the subject. The author would be happy to find these unpretending papers had created a greater interest among Englishmen in the condition of his country.

SWANSEA,

MARCH 28, 1867.

CONTENTS.

ERRATUM.

Page 47, line 10, instead of "Pædio Baptists" and "Anti-pædio Baptists,"
read "Pædobaptists" and "Anti-pædobaptists."

MISCELLANEOUS PAPERS, &c.

THE RESOURCES OF WALES.

A LECTURE DELIVERED AT THE ROYAL INSTITUTION OF SOUTH
WALES, SWANSEA, JANUARY THE 29TH, 1866.

WALES, though but a comparatively small portion of Great
Britain, its area, including Monmouthshire, being only
5,102,858 statute acres, is, owing to its exhaustless stores of
those material resources upon which the greatness of England
chiefly depends, incomparably more important than any other
district of the island of equal extent.

The scenery of the Principality is remarkable for grandeur,
variety, and beauty. Any one with an eye and a heart to
admire the wondrous works of the Creator, would be well
remunerated for the time and expense of a leisurely tour
through Wales. Setting out from Chepstow, and following the
coast through all its curves and windings by Newport, Cardiff,
Swansea, Kidwelly, Laugharne, Tenby, Pembroke, Milford,
St. David's, Cardigan, Aberystwyth, Barmouth, Carnarvon,
Holyhead, Amlwch, and Beaumaris to Flint: the tourist will
then turn to view the interior of the country, when of course
he will not be able to resist the temptation to ascend the
highest peaks of Snowdon, Carnedd Llewellyn, Carnedd
Dafydd, Cadair Idris, Aranfawddwy, Plinlimmon, the Brecon
and Carmarthenshire Beacons, the Frenny-fawr and Pencwm-
cerwyn. Descending from those high elevations, he will
naturally wish to traverse the Vale of Glamorgan—"the.
Garden of Wales;" the ever-green fields and meadows along
the banks of the Usk, the Wye, the Severn, the Towy, and
the Teivi; to have a full sight of the celebrated Vale of Clwyd
from Corwen to Rhyl, and to notice with care every interesting object in the picturesque valleys of Aeron, Ystwyth,
Rheidol, Meivod, Llangollen, Llanrwst, and Maentwrog. At

B

several of these places, barren mountains, high cliffs, and fertile fields are to be seen at one view. If such a sight would not fill the coldest and the dullest mind with lively and sublime poetical ideas, nothing else could.

The surface of Wales has some things still more substantial and valuable than grand and varied scenery to please the eye and enliven the mind. The rich soil of its sheltered valleys produces luxuriant crops and feeds multitudes of cattle; thousands of acres of the declivities of its hills and the sides of its narrow dingles—too steep for cultivation, are adorned by millions of valuable oak, ash, alder, and other useful trees; higher up on the mountains, where no tree will grow, hundreds of beautiful ponies are bred, and myriads of sheep, which supply our markets with the most delicious Welsh mutton, and the shops of our woollen-drapers with the finest Welsh flannel; whilst the numerous rivers and streams abound with the finest salmon, trout, and almost every other variety of fresh-water fish. Hilly, barren, and worthless as many districts of our country may appear, there is scarcely a spot from the top of its bleakest mountains to the rocky beds of its most rapid rivulets, which does not produce something or other for the comfort and sustenance of man. An enumeration of those good things for which Wales is noted would be incomplete without a reference to the remarkable salubrity of its air, and the superior quality of its abundant supply of water. Neither should we omit to mention its celebrated medicinal waters at Taff's Well, Llanwrtyd, Llangamarch, Builth, Llandrindod, Holywell, and Trefriw. Thousands of invalids and afflicted persons resort to these places every year, and now, having been made more accessible by railways, still larger numbers from all parts of the United Kingdom will be able to avail themselves of these provisions of our beneficent Creator for the alleviation of human suffering. Our neighbours, the English, are proverbially partial to everything Welsh, and sharp-sighted tradesmen turn that partiality to the best account. One could hardly pass through any street in London, and other English cities, without seeing on signs and in shop-windows, in bold, legible characters, "Excellent Welsh mutton, superior Welsh flannel, genuine Welsh ale, pure Welsh bread," &c. Keen and business-like as Englishmen generally are, yet it is highly probable that they are often imposed upon, and that they consume vast quantities of pretended Welsh commodities which never came from Wales.

Notwithstanding all the attractions of its scenery, the salubrity of its air and water, together with the variety and value of the productions of its soil, Wales would have remained for ever a comparatively unknown and unimportant district of Great Britain, had it not been for its boundless store of valuable minerals of every description. It is that which constitutes its incalculable importance; which opens before it a glorious prospect; and which will make it for centuries to come, as far as material resources are concerned, the main pillar upon which the superiority of England among the nations of the world is to rest. It is not probable that any tract of country, of equal extent, in any part of the known World, contains such a quantity and variety of minerals as Wales. In an enumeration of these hidden treasures of our rocks, our coal demands the first place, for without this essential article every other mineral would have been of little use.

The great coal-field of South Wales is said to be the largest in Europe, and with the exception of that of Nova Scotia, to contain a greater vertical thickness of strata than any coal-field in the world. It extends from Pontypool, in Monmouthshire, on the east, to St. Bride's Bay, in Pembrokeshire, on the west, a distance of about ninety miles. Its average breadth is from twelve to thirteen miles. The area is calculated by Mr. Joshua Richardson, of Neath, at 1,055 square miles; and by Mr. Edward Hull, author of "the Coal-fields of Great Britain," at 1,094. This immense field contains no less than sixty-four seams of coal, varying in thickness from one foot to eighteen, and even twenty feet. The aggregate thickness of all these seams is 190 feet and 10 inches; but as several of the veins do not extend through the whole field, it is impossible to say what is the precise average thickness of the coal. Mr. Martin, whose paper on the South Wales coal-field is the authority generally referred to, estimates the average thickness of the workable coal throughout the whole area at 95 feet, and he calculates that each square mile, after deducting one third for waste ground and loss in working, will produce 64,000,000 of tons. According to this estimate the produce of the whole field would amount to the enormous quantity of seventy thousand millions of tons. Mr. Hussey Vivian's estimate does not exceed thirty-six thousand millions, while that of Mr. Edward Hull is as low as twenty-six thousand millions. But even according to the lowest of these estimates, the South Wales field alone would supply the whole kingdom with coal at the rate of one hundred millions of tons a-year for above two hundred and sixty years. The produce of our coal-field, in the year 1864, was eleven millions of tons. If our own consumption and export trade were doubled, our resources are amply sufficient to supply our need for nearly a thousand years, according to Mr. Hull's estimate; and for three thousand years according to Mr. Martin's estimate.

The South Wales coal-field is celebrated not only on account of the vast quantity of coal which it contains, but also on account of its variety and superior quality. The coals of this field are divided into five different classes : the bituminous, the semi-bituminous, the partially-bituminous, the anthracitous, and the anthracite. These different kinds of coal have their respective uses, and add to the value of the field which supplies the markets of the world with them. The number of collieries in South Wales and Monmouthshire is 418.

South Wales is not the only coal-producing district of the Principality. There are three coal fields in North Wales, in the counties of Denbigh, Flint, and Anglesea, whose area is one hundred and eleven square miles. The coal raised in North Wales last year (1864), amounted to nearly two millions of tons (1,987,060). The number of collieries is 81. Mr. Hull says that the Flintshire coal field will be exhausted in about forty or fifty years at the present rate of consumption ; but he estimates the workable coal in the Denbighshire field at nine hundred and three millions of tons;—a sufficient quantity to last for above three centuries, were the consumption of the North Wales district to rise one-third above its present rate, exclusive of what remains in the coal fields of Flintshire and Anglesea, which probably amounts to twenty-seven or thirty millions of tons.

The mineral which ranks next to coal in point of practical value is iron ore, and happily Wales is richly stored with it. The argillaceous or clay iron stone, which has hitherto been chiefly used in the iron works of Wales, is found in regular beds or veins interstratified with the coal measures. The aggregate thickness of the veins in the lower series of the coal strata, is about five feet, and the carbonaceous ore, or "black band," which is found chiefly in the upper coal series, is from eighteen to thirty-six inches thick. It is calculated that each square mile of the coal field contains eleven millions of tons of argillaceous and carbonaceous iron ore. Several beds of calcareous hæmatite ore are to be found in the carboniferous

limestone on the south anticlinal line of the coal field from
Pontypool to Lydstep Point, in Pembrokeshire. These valuable ores are at present but very partially examined, but
further search will probably lead to new discoveries. The
red hæmatite of the Permian series is also found in several
districts outside the southern extremity of the coal field. It
is now largely worked at Llantrisant, Wenvoe, and other
places in Glamorganshire. The authors of the "Memoirs of
the geological survey of Great Britain" remark "that the
iron ores of South Wales are not yet developed so rapidly as
to satisfy the requirements of the trade. Nearly 400,000
tons per annum of iron ores are imported from the Lancashire
and Whitehaven districts in the north of England, and also
large supplies are obtained from the south and west of
England, Spain, Elba, and other foreign ports. The superior
quality of the *coal* for smelting purposes seems to give this
district an advantage which compensates for the want of very
cheap iron ores. The iron ores in the South Wales district
are not yet fully understood and developed; but the stubborn
fact remains that with 25 cwt. of raw coal they can, and do
when properly used, make a ton of pig-iron." The quantity
of iron ore raised in South Wales in 1864 was 468,355 tons
and 5 cwts., of the value of £185,360 17s. 1d. The average
yield of the argillaceous ore is about 36 per cent. of iron, and
that of the hæmatite from 47 to 49 per cent. There are also
in the coal districts of North Wales and their vicinities
several beds of argillaceous and hæmatite ores; 29,127 tons
were raised there in 1864, valued at £9,835 12s. 6d.

There are exhaustless beds of lead and silver ores in almost
every county of the Principality. The lead mines of Cardiganshire have been worked from the time of Henry VIII. to the
present day. As early as the seventeenth century they
yielded enormous profits to their proprietors. Sir Hugh
Middleton, who worked them for some years, realised a nett
profit of £20,000 a-year, which, in his time, was six or seven
times the value of such a sum in this age. The produce of the
Cardiganshire mines in the year 1864 amounted to 7464 tons
of ore of the value of £106,362. Lead and silver mines are
also extensively worked in the counties of Flint, Denbigh,
and Montgomery, and on a smaller scale in Pembrokeshire,
Carmarthenshire, Breconshire, Merionethshire, ahd, Carnarvonshire. When the railways which are now in course of
formation in each of these counties are completed, the vast

mineral resources of the country will soon be greatly developed, which is but very partially the case at present. There are now in Wales no less than 300 mines, in which lead, silver, and other ores are worked. The lead ore produce of these mines last year was 27,146 tons, which yielded 19,509 tons of lead, and 136,885 ounces of silver.

Parys Mountain, in Anglesea, has been for ages celebrated for its copper ore. The produce of that mountain last year was 7857 tons of ore. Small quantities of copper are also raised in the counties of Carnarvon, Merioneth, Montgomery, Cardigan, and Brecknock. The total produce of the copper mines of Wales in the year 1864 was 9533 tons, estimated to contain 613 tons of pure copper, of the value of £61,300.

The various mines of the counties of Cardigan, Carmarthen, Denbigh, Flint, and Carnarvon, have produced 4238 tons of zinc ore in the year 1864, or nearly one-third of the entire produce of the United Kingdom in that year. The value of this ore amounts to £16,177. The mines of North Wales have also in 1864 produced 1975 tons of sulphur ore, of the value of £1,264; 2,153 tons of ochre of the value of £2,045, and 833 tons of blue stone—a valuable mineral, containing copper, zinc, lead, and silver—were raised in the Anglesea copper mines last year.

The rocks of Wales contain not only coal, iron, lead, copper, zinc, and silver, but also gold. Gold mining in Wales is as yet in its infancy. It was only about six years ago that the first attempt to open a gold mine was made; but such is the attraction of the precious metal that now we find in a limited district of Merionethshire no less than twenty-one mines opened. Mr. Readwin, of Manchester, in a paper read before the British Association for the Advancement of Science, at Birmingham, last September, gives us the most cheering account of the prospects of Welsh gold mining. "Gold mining in Wales," he remarks, "has gone now very far beyond experimental trials. More than seven thousand tons of quartz have been operated upon, and more than thirteen thousand ounces of gold obtained therefrom, worth say £50,000, averaging more than 36 dwts. to the ton. With half a ton of gold as the result, I challenge the boldest objector to gold mining in Wales, as a branch of industry, to prove that it cost one-half of £50,000 to obtain it. After several years of experimental effort to work the gold minerals of Merioneth at a profit, I am more fixed in my opinion than ever, notwith-

standing the equivocal position the subject holds as a
commercial pursuit, that gold mining can and will be made
remunerative, if certain essential and natural conditions
prevails at the respective mines:—Firstly, there must be a
large and continuous quantity of the auriferous mineral,
cheaply obtainable by means of adits and tramways; secondly,
there must be efficient water-power available on the spot;
thirdly, there must be no more cats about the premises than
will catch mice. Under such circumstances, provided 40 or
50 tons of minerals can be raised per diem, a quarter of an
ounce of gold to the ton ought to pay all costs of reduction,
and I think it would!" The workmen at these mines, while
searching for gold, have discovered very rich lead, silver,
copper, and zinc ores. These may ultimately prove much
more remunerative than the gold itself.

Wales abounds with immense beds of the finest building
and paving stone in the world, which outcrop on the declivities of the hills through the length and breadth of the country,
and might be quarried at a comparatively trifling expense.
These useful materials were not created in vain. The time
will come when they shall be turned to some good account.
Thousands of tons of the hard blue stone of Penmaenmawr
and Nevin, in Carnarvonshire, are annually conveyed to
England and several foreign countries; the fine flags of South
Wales, which are capable of being cut into blocks of any
dimensions, will some time or other attract the attention of
the world. Neither should we omit to mention that exhaustless quantities of the finest fire-clay are to be found in almost
every district of the Principality, especially the mining districts.

The last mineral I shall name, for which Wales is so celebrated, and which ranks next to coal and iron ore as an important
marketable commodity and a source of wealth to the community, is slate. The mountains of Carnarvonshire, Merionethshire, and some districts of the counties of Denbigh, Montgomery, Carmarthen, and Pembroke abound with immense
beds of the finest slate rocks in the world. Formerly slates
were only used for covering the roofs of houses, but now they
are brought into an almost endless variety of purposes, such as
cisterns, chimney-pieces, paving, and all sorts of fancy
ornaments. It is said that the utility of the Carnarvonshire
slates was discovered as early as the time of Queen Elizabeth,
but it does not seem that any use had been made of them
further than for roofing a few houses in the immediate neigh-

bourhoods of the quarries, till the early part of the last
century. A young woman named Elizabeth Griffiths drove a
pony, which carried the first load of slates for shipment to the
port of Bangor, in the year 1715. Notwithstanding the
decided superiority of slate to every other material as a neat,
light, and durable covering for the roofs of buildings, a considerable number of years elapsed before the public, who
usually cling with stupid tenacity to old customs, would allow
it to replace unsightly and combustible thatch and clumsy
tiles. As late as the year 1772 the clear annual profit of the
Penrhyn quarry, almost the only slate quarry then worked in
Wales, was only £40, but at present that quarry, which is
certainly the largest in the world, is said to yield to its proprietor the princely income of £120,000 a year. The Llan-
beris quarries rank next to the Penrhyn, and are said to be
yielding the annual profits of £70,000. The annual income
of the late Lord Palmerston's quarries at Festiniog is from
£30,000 to £40,000. Besides these gigantic works there are
forty or fifty other slate quarries in Wales, chiefly in the
counties of Carnarvon and Merioneth, where thousands of
workmen are employed. About 14,000 men are employed in
the slate quarries of the Principality, exclusive of carriers,
railway men, and hundreds of labourers at the different ports
where the slates are shipped, and it is calculated that not less
than 600,000 tons of slates are sent to the market every year,
which at the present average price of fifty shillings per ton
amount to one million and a half sterling. This important
branch of Welsh industry is as yet only in its infancy. The endless quantity of slate veins which our mountains contain, the
superiority of Welsh slate to every other material of the same
nature yet discovered in any part of the world, the ever
increasing demand, which more than doubles the supply,
together with the enormous profits which the owners of Welsh
slate quarries derive from them, will most certainly soon
induce capitalists to join practical Welsh quarrymen to open
new works and enlarge existing ones. The probability is
that the markets of the world will be supplied twenty years
hence with treble the present quantity of slate, and what a
source of wealth will that be to the landed proprietors, the
working classes, and the community at large?
    The Principality is not only famous for its mineral wealth,
but equally so also on account of the facilities which its
geographical position furnish for the easy transit of its mineral,

and all other productions to the market. The bulk of its minerals is found within fifteen or twenty miles of one or the other of our convenient seaports, and the numerous valleys which stretch out in different directions from the extremities of the mining districts to the ports, show that the Creator has adapted this country to be the scene of unparalleled manufacturing and commercial greatness. The time cannot be very distant when it will be seen that it was a glaring mistake to select the plains of Lancashire, with their dirty and stagnant waters, as the head quarters of British manufactories, with the dangerous port of Liverpool as the outlet, when nature had pointed South Wales with its hundreds of ever-running crystal streams, its endless supply of coal and iron, and all in the vicinity of Milford Haven, the finest, the safest, and the most capacious port in Europe, as the proper home of British industry. The enormous capital laid out in Lancashire may for some time stand in the way of the commercial progress of Wales, and the erection of cotton mills and other manufactories in the inviting valleys of the Teivi, the Towy, the Cothi, &c., but neither art, wealth, nor prejudice can for ever compete with nature. Here the manufacturer would have his choice of water or steam power to work his machineries; and would not at any time of the year be in want of the one or the other, provided his mills were built in the right places.

The mineral resources of the country have brought into existence manufactories of gigantic magnitude for the smelting and the manufacturing of the different metals which our mines produce.

The Iron Works of South Wales are carried on on a very extensive scale. It is evident that the Romans when they invaded the island, constructed furnaces for smelting iron in South Wales, and it is very probable that iron smelting was carried on here to some extent during the middle ages. In the reign of Queen Elizabeth some of the Sussex iron masters established iron works in the counties of Monmouth and Glamorgan, but charcoal was the only fuel used for smelting the ore until late in the last century. The make of iron was consequently very limited. Dr. Thomas Llewellyn, in a book published in the year 1768, says that the iron manufactured then in Wales was scarcely sufficient to make ploughshares and shoes for the horses. When coke came into general use instead of charcoal, and steam instead of water power to furnish blast for the furnaces, an impetus was given to iron

c

smelting, and it has ever since rapidly progressed. We find that the entire produce of all the furnaces of Glamorganshire in the year 1796 was only 16,304 tons of pig-iron; in 1820 it amounted to 49,980 tons; in 1830 to 81,258 tons; in 1840 to 132,002 tons; in 1846 to 243,616 tons; and in 1864 to 481,822 tons. The progress of the works in the adjoining counties during the same period was somewhat similar. There are at present in the Principality 52 iron works with 211 furnaces, 141 of which are in blast, and their total produce of pig-iron in the year 1864 was 988,729 tons; connected with these works there are 39 forges and mills, containing 1,413 puddling furnaces, and 164 rolling mills. More than four-fifths of the total quantity of rails annually exported from Great Britain are manufactured in South Wales, and shipped at Newport, Cardiff, Swansea, and Llanelly; lare quantities of rails and other descriptions of manufactured iron are also sent by rail from Wales to Liverpool for shipment.

Another branch of British industry, of which Wales has almost the entire monopoly, is copper smelting. Our respected townsman, Major Francis, has shown that copper smelting was commenced at Neath as early as the year 1584. This like iron smelting has progressed from age to age until it has attained the present gigantic scale on which it is carried on. 7,000 tons was the estimated annual amount of copper smelted in this country from British and foreign ores about the commencement of the present century. The annual production amounted to 28,000 tons in the year 1848. In that year the heavy and restrictive duty imposed upon copper ores was removed. In consequence of that the copper trade extended rapidly. The present annual production in the United Kingdom is about 50,000 tons, 43,000 of which are smelted in Swansea and the surrounding district, from Port Talbot on the east, to Pembrey on the west. The copper trade has always been less fluctuating than the iron trade, and consequently the populations dependent upon it are less exposed to privations and unfavourable changes than those of the iron districts.

Wales has nearly monopolized the manufacture of tin-plates as well as the smelting of copper. The most extensive manufactories in the world are situate in the counties of Glamorgan, Monmouth, and Carmarthen. There are in these three counties no less than 27 tin-plate works, containing 81 mills, and the estimated weekly make is 27,000 boxes, or

1,404,000 annually. Above 300,000 tons of coal and charcoal are annually consumed at these works.

Lead and silver smelting is also carrried on very extensively at Bagillt in Flintshire, and in the Swansea district. I have not been able to ascertain what proportion of the lead and silver produce of the United Kingdom is smelted in Wales, but it is highly probable that it greatly exceeds one-half of the whole.

It would be too tedious to give a minute account of all the small works where zinc and other metals are smelted and manufactured.* These establishments, though insignificant in comparison to the iron, copper, and tin-plate works, furnish employment and profit to hundreds of people, and their existence in Wales is owing to the abundant supply of coal with which our highly favoured country is so richly stored.

The development of the mineral resources of the Principality has progressed with astonishing rapidity since the commencement of the present century, especially within the last thirty years, and the probability is that it will progress with still greater rapidity within the next thirty years. The extension of the coal and iron trade about the close of the last century necessitated the formation of canals for the transit of the productions of the mining and manufacturing districts into the ports. These were afterwards supplemented by tramroads, but both in the course of a few years proved inadequate to the requirements of the rapidly growing trade. In the year 1840 the Taff Vale Railway—the first railway in Wales, was opened. Since the opening of the Taff Vale other railways have been formed throughout South and North Wales. At present we have no less than 800 miles of railway in the Principality, and three or four hundred miles more will be opened in the course of the next five years. The capital invested in the railways already opened amounts at least to twenty millions. Docks, harbours, and other conveniences of shipping have also been constructed at every port in the Bristol Channel from Newport to Pembrey, at an enormous outlay. The aggregate of the capital invested in South Wales within the last seventy years in mines, manufactories, canals, tramroads, railways, docks, and all the other requirements of a gigantic trade, is almost beyond computation, but the ample resources of the district are such as to secure to every investor profitable returns wherever the capital is wisely invested and

honestly managed.   The present annual value of the mineral
productions of Wales may be thus estimated:—

Coal exported and sent by rail to England	£3,000,000
Iron	6,000,000
Copper	4,300,000
Tin-plates.	1,750,000
Slates	1,500,000
Lead, silver, gold, zinc, &c.	500,000
	£17,050,000

After deducting from the above, say three millions and fifty
thousand pounds for the copper-ore, the iron-ore, and the
block-tin imported from England, the Colonies, and foreign
countries, we have the noble sum of fourteen millions as the
annual income of the mineral resources of Wales.   This vast
amount is distributed among the workmen, the tradesmen, the
owners of lands, mines, manufactories, and the railway, canal,
and dock companies of the district.

In reviewing the foregoing statements, it cannot fail to
strike the mind of every thoughtful person that the working men of Wales are doomed to hard labour—to dangerous and exhaustive employments in mining, smelting, and
preparing the metals, while the lighter and more remunerative
labour of converting those metals into an endless variety of
marketable articles, is monopolized by the skilful artisans and
mechanics of England.   We find in the census returns that 12
per cent. of the adult male population of England are artisans
and mechanics, while hardly five per cent of the male population of Wales are so described.   This is not as it should be.
There is no reason in the world why the poor Welsh workman,
more than others, should expose himself to fatal explosions and
accidents in mines, or roast himself at the smelting furnace, to
prepare materials for the comparatively light and remunerative
employments of cutlers, gold, silver, and copper smiths, in England.   Some, of course, must perform the hard and dangerous
work, but light and heavy work should be carried on in the same
localities, and divided, as far as possible, among the members
of the same families.   How, then, is this inequality to be
rectified ?   Not, of course, by Acts of Parliament, nor by any
scheme set on foot by the employers of labour, but by the
workmen themselves.   Young men, if you wish to rise in the
world, to be the honour of your families and country, and to
have light work and high wages, you must abstain from those

gross and grovelling pleasures which the beershop offers you, and also from the effeminate and time-killing amusements of concerts, theatres, and frivolous parties, and apply yourselves with diligence and determination to the study of the arts and the sciences, and the cultivation of a refined taste in mechanics. Drudgery and heavy labour are proper punishments for those who have talent for higher employments, but neglect to cultivate it.

No country under the sun holds out a better prospect than Wales for those who have talent and taste for the employments of mining districts. Poor farmers, who groan under high rents and heavy taxes, and cannot pay their way, could not do better for themselves and their families than emigrate to the United States, or one of the Colonies; but the able miner who emigrates from his native country to follow the same occupation elsewhere, acts the part of a madman. It would be no exaggeration to say that sober, industrious, and prudent young men could rise from the ranks of the working-class to wealth and social respectability, and even to be millionaires, without crossing the borders of Wales.

It would be difficult thoughtfully to contemplate the future of Wales without a mixed feeling of joy and serious apprehension. It is evident to every one that observes the signs of the times, that the population and the trade of the mining districts of Wales will increase probably four fold before the close of the present century. And what effect will this sudden and rapid increase have on the social, the moral, and the religious condition of the community? Are our educational, charitable, and religious institutions in so flourishing and efficient a state, and capable of such immediate extension as to supply the wants, not only of the present population, but also of thousands more to be soon added to them, and those not of the most cultivated and moral from the lower classes of England and Ireland? I fear this question cannot be answered in the affirmative. Is it not too true that the religious organizations of all sects do not but to a very limited extent beneficially influence the masses, and are not our schools too few in number, and in many instances glaringly inefficient? Ministers of religion, landed proprietors, employers of labour, and philanthropists universally should prepare themselves for more energetic efforts than ever for the promotion of the intellectual, moral, and religious improvement of the working classes, otherwise the extension of our trade and the increase of our population instead of being a blessing, will turn out to be an awful curse to our beloved Wales. May God forbid that carelessness, covetousness, or religious exclusiveness and bigotry should be permitted to prevent our hearty and united co-operation for the moral and religious welfare of our country.

THE WORKING CLASSES OF WALES.

A LECTURE DELIVERED AT THE ROYAL INSTITUTION OF SOUTH WALES, SWANSEA, FEBRUARY THE 1ST, 1864.

THE working classes of Wales, like every other class of the great human family, have their peculiarities. Owing to the great influx of English, Scotch, and Irish labourers to the coal and iron districts of the counties of Glamorgan, Monmouth, Denbigh, and Flint, within the last forty years, the peculiar characteristics of the Welsh labourer are to a great extent, obliterated in those counties. We must therefore turn to the agricultural districts and the neighbourhoods of the slate quarries of North Wales in order to find communities of Welsh workmen in their genuine native character. The labouring classes of Wales, wherever they are to be found without any admixture of foreign elements and habits, are characterised by several very commendable qualities. As a class of people they are remarkable for their loyalty and sub-mission to their superiors. Ever since the incorporation of Wales with England, the loyalty of the Welsh nation to their Saxon rulers has been perfectly unswerving, notwithstanding the occasional effusions of frenzied poets and hot-headed orators against the Saxon invaders. Who has ever heard, from the days of Henry VIII. to the present hour, of secret clubs and traitorous plots in Wales to upset the Government, such as have from time to time disgraced Ireland?

Whatever view may be entertained of the unhappy conflicts between Charles I. and the Parliament, the Welsh, almost to a man, sided with the King until they were forced to sub-mission by the victorious arms of the Parliament. If their adherence to the Royal cause does not prove their attachment to

Protestantism and religious liberty, it proves, to say the least, their determined loyalty. And the various and important political, social, and religious changes of the last two hundred and forty years have not in any sense lessened, but vastly increased the loyalty of the Welsh people. Queen Victoria has not in any part of her wide dominion a million of more attached and loyal people than her warm-hearted Welsh subjects. This remark is quite as applicable to the working classes as to the middle and the upper classes. The lower classes in Wales are so far from conducting themselves with rudeness and disrespect . towards their superiors, that they almost run to the opposite extreme of idolizing them. No landowner, proprietor of works, nor any other member of the upper class in the Principality, has cause to fear the dagger of the assassin, the fire of the incendiary, or the rude assaults of an infuriated mob. The very rare instances of misunderstanding between small tenant farmers and their landlords, or workmen and their employers, which occur now and then, are almost invariably to be traced to the insolence and tyranny of agents, rather than to a spirit of insubordination in the people. Whatever may be the defects of the Welsh peasantry, the most ungrudging and cheerful submission to their superiors forms a prominent feature of their character. Even one of the Education Commissioners, in spite of all his inveterate prejudice against the Welsh people, was forced to acknowledge "that there is in the miners of South Wales but little of that dogged, desperate, wrong-headed courage which distinguishes the English miner." The working classes of Wales, including the small tenant farmers, who are generally worse off than the generality of our labourers, are exemplary for their industry, frugality, and quiet endurance of the most distressing poverty. I have no wish to conceal the fact that we have among our labouring classes numerous and sad examples of extravagance, improvidence, and inexcusable carelessness; but these, numerous as they are, are the exceptions, not the rule. The bulk of our working population are economical, industrious, and commendably provident. I know a man, who, for the last thirty years, has cultivated a small farm of about thirty-five acres, in the most bleak and mountainous district of this country, for which he pays the high rent of £35 a year. On that barren spot he has brought up thirteen healthy children without any other means of supporting his large family than the scanty produce of his small barren farm. Of course it was quite out of the question for him to pay for the education of his children, as he had to tax all his ingenuity to find them the bare necessaries of life, but in a neighbouring Sunday-school they were taught gratuitously to read their Bibles, and they have all grown up to be virtuous young men and women, worthy of their industrious parents. This is only one instance out of hundreds of similar ones which are to be found in different parts of the Principality.

As a further illustration of the rigid economy which the lower classes in Wales are compelled to observe, I beg leave to introduce the following incident:—The late Sir Robert Vaughan, of Nannau, Merionethshire, some years ago, accompanied by two or three gentlemen, went to the mountains to shoot grouse. Having gone further than they at first intended, and when at a distance of eight or ten miles from any place where they might get refreshment, they turned to the first house they could come to, which happened to be a small farm-house, or rather a hut, on the mountain side, to get something to eat, as they felt very hungry. There they found a girl of about thirteen years of age, and a boy of eleven years, with a number of younger children, the parents having gone from home that day. They asked for some food, and the girl, having not the remotest idea who the strangers were, brought to the table a jugful of buttermilk and a loaf of barley-bread, as black as the peat they used for fuel. One of the strangers enquired whether they had any butter in the house. "Yes," was the reply, "we have, but we are not allowed to take it, except on Sundays.". When they insisted on having some butter with the bread, the boy, in the most heroic manner, ran out and brought in a spade, threatening, to the no small amusement of the gentlemen, to strike the first of them who would dare to touch their butter; "for," said he, "we must keep and sell it all to get money to pay the rent to Sir Robert Vaughan." It is said that Sir Robert, the following day, ordered his agent to reduce the rent of that small farm 40 or 50 per cent. Hundreds of our sober and frugal workmen in the manufacturing, and some in the agricultural districts, are the owners of their own snug little cottages, and many more might be, were it not for their carelessness and intemperance. It is not probable that there is a community of working men to be found in any district of the United Kingdom equal to the working men of Wales for

economy, industry, and the observance of those personal and
social virtues which are essential to domestic happiness and
the well-being of society at large, though the wages of workmen
are, on an average, from eight to ten per cent. lower in Wales
than in England and Scotland.

Our working classes are also decidedly superior in their
morality to the corresponding classes in England and other
parts of the kingdom. Prejudiced parties have repeatedly
represented the people of Wales as deeply sunk in immorality,
and as destitute of any sense of moral obligation. I do not
stand here as a special pleader for my countrymen, and
God forbid that I should utter a word of apology for any
kind of immorality. The morality of Wales, when compared
with the requirements of the Divine Law, is deplorably low,
but when compared with the morality of England, Scotland,
and Ireland, it stands very high. According to the Judicial
Statistics for the year ending September 29, 1860, the number
of all the persons committed for different crimes in the twelve
Welsh counties, was 3,774, or about one to every 294 of the
population; while 112,508 were committed in England, or
one to every 168 of the population. The number of prisoners
convicted in Wales was 410, or one to every 2,711 of the
population, while the number of convicts in England amounted
to 11,658, or about one to every 1,628 of the population.
The Judicial Statistics also record another fact, which tells
greatly in favour of the natives of Wales. Of the 3,774
committed in the Principality, 791 were natives of England,
612 were Irishmen, 59 were Scotchmen, 32 were natives of
the Colonies, 110 were foreigners, and 47 were persons whose
birthplaces had not been ascertained. These facts speak for
themselves. The proportion of criminals to the population in
Wales is full 40 per cent. less than in England; and of those
criminals who disgrace the Principality, nearly one-half are
not natives, while the proportion of the natives to the other
inhabitants is at least nine to one. Out of every thousand
persons committed in England and Wales for the year 1860,
only twenty-five were natives of the Principality, which is
one-half less, in proportion to the population, than the average
for the whole of England and Wales. We thus see that the
people of Wales are, in their morals, as far as criminal statistics prove the point, twice as good as the people of England.
But, after all, the great question is, not whether we are better
than other people, but whether we are what we should be.

D

Rather than indulge in a vainglorious boasting of our superiority to others, let us all unite, heart and hand, to wipe off all the foul spots which still disgrace the character of the nation.

The crowning glory of the working classes of Wales, and the source of all their other commendable qualities, is their regard for religion. While I cannot say that anything like a majority of our working population are decidedly pious, I can safely state that five-sixths of them are frequent attendants at places of religious worship. Swansea, Cardiff, with some smaller towns and villages on the borders of the English counties, may furnish exceptions to this almost universal rule. The population of the iron and coal districts of Wales, mixed and anglicised as it is, forms a glorious contrast to the corresponding districts in the counties of Warwick, Stafford, Lancaster, York, and Durham. In the Welsh districts, a stranger would see through the smoke and dust large and conspicuous places of worship overtowering the workmen's cottages, and on Sundays he might observe thousands of decently clad people flocking to their respective sanctuaries, while in the English districts the most prominent buildings are the gin palaces; the spire of a church is to be seen here and there, and a few Wesleyan and Primitive Methodist chapels are to be found, but generally in obscure corners. These houses of prayer are chiefly attended by the middle class, while the bulk of the working class are to be seen by the hundreds on a summer Sunday morning, half dressed and unwashed, lounging about the doors of their cottages reading a Sunday newspaper, or standing in groups at the corners of the streets waiting the hour for the beer-shops to be opened. I never felt more thankful to God for the prevalence of religion among the working classes of Wales than I did some four years ago, during a tour through the English iron and coal districts, when I had an opportunity of observing the remarkable contrast between the two districts. The working classes of Wales are, happily, neither the dupes of infidel pedants, like too many in the corresponding classes in England, nor priest-ridden and grossly superstitious like the Irish; but the bulk of them are respectably well-informed Protestants. Still, it is a matter of deep regret that a considerable number of them—probably one-sixth—seldom or never attend any place of religious worship, while a lamentably large proportion of those who are regular attendants and intelligent men are far from conforming in principle and practice to the rules of that religion which teacheth us to deny ungodliness and worldly lust, and to live soberly, righteously, and godly in this present world.

Our working classes, whatever may be their excellencies, are also characterised by some glaring faults, and honesty requires that they should be pointed out. One very prominent fault of our working men is their readiness to allow themselves to be made the dupes of cunning and designing men. Several instances of this have occurred in the counties of Monmouth and Glamorgan within the last thirty-five years. About the year 1833, a cunning Englishman named Twist, who pretended to be a most sincere friend of the working classes, visited Merthyr and other places on the Hills, where he induced thousands of the people to form themselves into a kind of Workingmen's Union for the professed purposes of defending their rights against the tyranny of the masters, and raise the price of labour by refusing to instruct any workmen from the agricultural districts in mining operations. The designing originator of the Union gained his object by securing to himself large sums of money from his dupes, but his plausible scheme led to nothing better than the horrid nocturnal doings of the *Scotch cattle*, and a series of ruinous strikes which brought hundreds of families to the very brink of starvation. The chartist movement in the year 1839 originated in a similar manner. A number of mob orators came down from England, who, by their thundering declamation against the oppression and injustice of the aristocracy, and fair promises of a perfect earthly paradise to the working classes as soon as the points of the charter would become the law of the land, soon gathered around their standard hundreds of confident expectants of the best things on earth. But, in the course of a few months all their high expectations ended in a disgraceful riot, poverty, imprisonment, and death.

It is also by designing characters that our working men are invariably led to unite in strikes. The promoters of strikes are not industrious workmen, but dissatisfied idlers, who seldom settle for any length of time under the same employer. They are very fluent and great talkers, pretending to be thoroughly accomplished politicians, and well versed in all the mysteries of trade. By describing in strong terms the injustice and the hardships to which the poor workman is subjected, the certainty of an advance of wages after a determined strike, and the glorious good times which would follow,

they entice a number of silly men to their nets; the plan is
formed, and those who may feel reluctant to join are frightened
to acquiescence. The strike commences, families soon begin
to be in want, the originators of the evil, having no character
to lose, nor any property to tie them to the locality, abscond,
leaving their dupes in the lurch. All the unhappy strikes
which have taken place in Wales from time to time originated
in this manner. We trust that our working population are,
from year to year, becoming wiser, and that babbling idlers
and designing characters shall not have as much influence over
them in the future as they had in the past.

  We should not omit to mention another defect which charac-
terises the Welsh working classes, viz., a want of refined taste
and a commendable aim to execute every work with neatness.
The English workman, as a rule, greatly excels the Welshman
in this respect. This does not arise from any want of skill in
the Welshman, for there are many Welshmen as skilful and tasty
as any Englishman in every branch of work, from the most
ordinary farming operation to the most ingenious engineering
achievement, but it is rather to be attributed to a notion which
has been, and which is still, we fear, too prevalent throughout the nation, that to devote time and labour to the execution
of any work with good taste and neatness, is an unnecessary
waste. We are accustomed to remark when we see any tool,
article of furniture, or building, of a more clumsy construction
or make than usual, "Why, this must be the work of a
Welshman." We trust, however, that this wrong notion is
gradually losing its hold on the national mind, and that our
working classes will not in future allow their English brethren
to excel them in anything which is praiseworthy.

  Our working classes are also very backward in general
knowledge. In religious knowledge they are incomparably
superior to the working classes in England, but in secular
education the English are far ahead of the Welsh. In the
last report of the Registrar General we find that out of every
hundred persons married in the Northern counties of England,
from 70 to 80 could write their names on the register, while
only from 60 to 65 could do it in Wales. Our day schools
are increasing in number and efficiency, but not by any means
in proportion to the wants of the country and the increase of
the population, which is at the rate of ten thousand a-year.

  Without qualifying anything I have advanced in favour of the
morality of our working classes, still it must be confessed that

vice in its various odious forms prevails to an alarming extent among them, especially the destructive habit of immoderate drinking. This is the root of almost all the ignorance, poverty, irreligion, and dishonesty in dealing, of which trades-men constantly complain. Were our working men persuaded to desert the beer-shops, they would be well able to support efficient schools for the education of their children, maintain the aged and the orphan, satisfy the demands of the shop-keepers, and thousands who never enter the door of a church or chapel, would be constant attendants on the ordinances of religion. This subject has been urged on the attention of our working men times without number with over-powering eloquence, but still thousands cling to their filthy and disgust-ing habits with the obstinacy of madmen. Still we are not to give them up as hopeless. Many have been reclaimed, and we may expect greater results from the prevalence of religion and education, the establishment of Provident Societies, and other useful and philanthropic schemes, which tend to improve the taste and elevate the feelings of the multitude.

What is to be done to improve the character and ameliorate the condition of our working population? This is a most important question. Before attempting to answer it, permit me to observe that neither schemes proposed, aided, or enforced by the legislature, nor all the labours of the ministers of religion, the promoters of education, and our active philanthropists, will be of any avail unless they strive in earnest to reform themselves. But wise and benevolent schemes are useful and necessary as inducements to the mul-titude to aim at self-reformation. Employers, and all other persons of influence, should use every available means, con-sistent with the personal liberty of the working man, to remove out of his way every temptation to imtemperance, and every inducement to carelessness and improvidence. Our wealthiest and most respectable proprietors of works now generally prohibit the opening of beer-shops in the immediate neighbourhoods of their works, and the employment of beer-house keepers as agents, but this is not the case everywhere. The managers of many collieries and other works are also publicans, and the consequences are generally disastrous to the morality of the workmen. Whenever, on the other hand, proprietors and their agents set their faces against drinking, sobriety and morality in general are the invariable con-sequences.

The truck system may be ranked next to the drinking system as most injurious to the comfort and the morality of the working man. In former years the keepers of truck-shops used to buy inferior goods, such as no other shopkeeper could have disposed of, and sell them to the workmen at seven or ten per cent. above the market prices. Such flagrant injustice is now, I believe, generally done away with, and good articles may be had at the truck-shops at the same prices as at other shops; but after all, the truck system, however fair it may be carried on, has a direct tendency to foster extravagance and improvidence in the working classes. When the working man has the bills of his grocer, draper, tailor, shoemaker, and others, to meet, he endeavours to study economy, but when he has a running account at the "company's shop," where he can get every thing he needs for food and clothing, he becomes careless, and having worked under the same employer for ten or twenty years, if he finds himself after all penniless or deep in debt, he loses his self-respect, becomes reckless, and closes his miserable career in poverty and disgrace. It would be a very rare occurrence to find a workman, employed where the truck system is in operation, saving money or becoming a house proprietor. The truck system also affects the interest of the working class most injuriously by depriving them of the advantage of associating with the middle class. Respectable tradesmen do not reside in the neighbourhoods of those iron and coal works where the truck system is enforced. The workmen in such localities are separated from the society of people better educated than themselves, and who would beneficially affect their manners and habits.

Employers would do incalculable good to their workmen were they everywhere to exert all their influence to suppress immorality and everything which has a tendency to debase and impoverish them. On the other hand, employers and persons of influence might greatly improve the condition and the moral character of the working classes, by promoting the establishment of provident and building societies, and by urging all, over whom they have influence, to deposit every shilling they could spare in such societies or Savings Banks. In doing so, they would not only benefit their workmen, but themselves as well. There is a Welsh proverb, "A poor master, woe unto the servant." This proverb reversed would be equally true, "A poor servant, woe unto the master." We would never hear of strikes and riots were the bulk of our working men the proprietors of their own cottages, or depositors in the Savings Banks. Employers of labour have too often entertained the absurd notion that indigent and uneducated workmen are more easily managed than the thrifty and enlightened.

We can never expect our working population to be what they should and might be until they are better educated. Education would open wide fields of usefulness and happiness before them, from which they are, in their present uneducated condition, excluded. Of late years we have had a vast deal of talk about educating the working classes, but very little comparatively is actually done to accomplish it. Some attribute the backward state of education in Wales to the existence of the Welsh language, but that is very doubtful. Those districts where the Welsh language once prevailed, and is now almost extinct, are the most imperfectly educated. Monmouthshire, as we can prove by statistics, where hardly one-fourth of the population speak Welsh, is as far behind the six counties of South Wales, in point of education, as those counties are behind the best educated English counties. The principal impediments to the progress of education in Wales are the religious jealousies and bigotry which are so prevalent throughout the nation. We are divided into four large parties, exclusive of minor sects. Neither of these parties can educate the nation without the co-operation of the others, and at present we have but a very faint prospect that that desirable co-operation will ever be secured. Is it not a matter of deep regret that religious disputes should be permitted to interfere with and hinder the education of the masses? No protestant party would object to the reading of the Bible and the inculcation of its morality in a day school. Why should any one insist for more? What are the ministers of religion, religious parents, and our numerous host of Sunday School teachers good for, if the teachers of day schools are expected to indoctrinate young children in all those nice points of divinity which divide one religious party from another? May that happy day soon dawn when all parties shall lay aside their narrowmindedness and bigotry, and unite as one man in promoting the mental and moral elevation of the working classes of Wales.

THE WORKING CLASSES OF WALES AND RELIGIOUS INSTITUTIONS.

(Re-printed from the Nonconformist, for December 26, 1866.)

WHILE it appears that the bulk of the working classes of England never attend the means of grace, and that a large proportion of them are avowed infidels, fully ninety per cent. of the corresponding classes in Wales regularly attend public worship, except in the large towns and the most Anglicised districts, and even in those localities at least seventy-five per cent. of the Welsh-speaking masses are frequent or constant attendants at one or the other of our places of worship. A century ago our working classes were quite as irreligious as those classes are now in England, and imcomparably more ignorant, but in the present day they are under the influence of religion to a far greater extent than the other classes of the community. As you are now endeavouring in England to solve the problem, how the working classes are to be won to religion, which has long ago been happily solved in Wales, it cannot fail to be interesting to you to know by what means we have attained the object which you wish to compass.

Among the means which have proved so successful in the evangelisation of the masses in Wales, *effective preaching* claims the first place. No nation in Christendom has, within the last two centuries, been blessed with a succession of abler and more efficient preachers than the Welsh, and their preaching, from age to age, has been eminently characterised by the following essential qualifications of successful and popular preaching :—

1. *Sound doctrine.* The total depravity of man by the fall; the atoning sacrifice of Christ as the sinner's sole ground of hope; the necessity of the Holy Spirit's work to change the depraved heart, with a holy conduct as the evidence of that inward work; the eternal condemnation of all the impenitent, and the eternal salvation of every believer, have invariably been the themes upon which all our successful preachers

dwelt. Attempts have occasionally been made by men of talent and reputed piety, to win certain classes by ignoring or explaining away such doctrines of revealed religion as were deemed most unpalatable to the carnal mind, but every attempt of the kind, however well meant, has always turned out a most glaring failure. The working classes of Wales have been evangelised by a faithful preaching of the Gospel, the whole Gospel, and nothing but the Gospel.

2. *Richness of thought.* Several of our great preachers, especially in former ages, might be justly charged with the want of that refinement and delicacy of expression which becomes the Christian pulpit, but not one of them could be charged with tantalising their crowded congregations with showy wordy nothings under the name of sermons, or with an endless repetition of stereotyped phrases and threadbare ideas. The bulky volumes of Owen, Manton, Charnock, Goodwin, Howe, and other divines of the same stamp, have found their way to the humble cottages of most of our Welsh preachers, and they faithfully embody in their sermons all the rich thoughts with which those valuable works abound. The practice of itinerant preaching which was so general in the Principality in past ages, and is kept up to a great extent even in the present day, has enabled preachers of the most ordinary talents to treat their hearers, on their occasional visits, to sermons loaded with sterling thoughts, which they could not possibly have done had they been obliged to address the same hearers every Sabbath throughout the year. Experience has taught us that the most ignorant and uncultivated hearers, as well as the educated and most refined, will not be attracted by sermons or religious addresses devoid of striking ideas and telling illustrations.

3. *Perspicuous style.* Welsh congregations, as well as congregations in other countries, have too often had to undergo the infliction of listening to abstruse reasoning and metaphysicald isquisitions, clothed in terms unintelligible to nine-tenths of the people; but the ministers who have been imprudent enough to adopt such a style of preaching, have invariably, in a short time, either preached themselves out of their pulpits, or the people out of their pews. Those preachers whose instrumentality have made Wales what it is religiously, have always been distinguished for the perspecuity of their style. They have happily succeeded in bringing down the great truths of the Bible to the capacities of the humblest and most

E

uneducated of their hearers, and to make the vision so plain
that he who ran might have read it.

4. *Animated delivery.* The Welsh nation has been aroused
from its spiritual stupor and ignorance by men of extraordinary
power and eloquence as public speakers, and an animated
delivery is still considered as essential to popular and efficient
preaching. Dull and heavy speakers, remarkable for other
redeeming qualities, have in many instances been useful and
highly respected as teachers of congregations gathered by
others, but such men have never been instrumental in arousing
and attracting the ignorant masses. As our congregations
expect heat as well as light in the discourses, the practice of
reading sermons has never been attempted with success, for
paper is an unsuitable material to carry fire.

5. *Earnestness, solemnity, and directness of appeal* have
also been prominent characteristics of the Welsh pulpit. In
the latter half of the last, and the beginning of the present
century, most of our preachers would leave their homes for
weeks and months every year, traversing the country through
the rains, floods, snow, and frost of winter, and the scorching
heat of summer, travelling twenty or thirty miles each day,
preaching two or three times, and often with no better enter-
tainment after their hard day's labour than a crust of barley
bread with a cup of milk, and a bed of straw at a labourer's
cottage to lie upon for the night. The remuneration which
they received for their service was generally barely sufficient
to defray their travelling expenses. The costly sacrifices and
self-denial of these good men gradually became known to all
classes throughout the community, and greatly helped to
make their pathetic and solemn appeals to the consciences of
their hearers powerful, and in thousands of instances quite
irresistible. Even their enemies were forced to acknowledge
that they were really in earnest, and that the spiritual welfare
of their countrymen, rather than their own worldly advantage,
was the great object they had in view. Their earnest labours
have been crowned with success. Three thousand Dissenting
houses of prayer for a population of a million and a quarter,
prove that the common people in Wales are to a greater extent
under the influence of religion than they probably are in
any other Protestant country in the world. If the sufferings
and privations which Welsh preachers in former ages had to
undergo do not fall to the lot of their successors in this age,
still it is to be hoped that we are partakers of a large portion
of the earnest spirit of our worthy predecessors.

Preaching in Wales has never, since the rise of Dissent, been regarded as the exclusive and peculiar work of ordained ministers and theological students, except at one period when religion was in a very declining state. Hundreds of pious laymen are usefully employed as preachers by every Dissenting denomination. After the subjugation of the Royalists by Oliver Cromwell in the year 1646, the Congregational Churches at Llanvaches and Mynyddislwyn, the only Nonconformist churches then existing in Wales, sent out seventeen of their most gifted members to traverse the country as itinerant preachers, and this is the first instance of lay preaching we have in the history of religion in Wales. These pious laymen, headed by seven or eight young Puritan clergymen, carried on the work of evangelisation so successfully that we find in the dark and then irreligious Wales no less than 106 preachers ejected or silenced by the Act of Uniformity in 1662. Early in the eighteenth century, we see that lay preaching had by some means or other fallen almost entirely into desuetude. The ministers of that age—the immediate successors of the confessors of 1662—were all thoroughly educated men, but most of them were remarkably cold and formal, and excessively jealous for their official dignity, and in their way quite as priestly as the rankest Puseyite of the present day. They regarded lay preaching as an infringement upon the rights of their office, and therefore set their faces against it. Educated and respectable as these ministers were, their congregations dwindled away and irreligion deluged the country while they were guarding their fantastic privileges.

At the outbreak of the Great Methodist Revival in 1735, lay preaching was again revived. The clerical Methodists, with as many Dissenting ministers as had caught the fire, encouraged every talented layman in their church to exercise his gifts as a preacher. That irregularity annoyed the formal Dissenting priests as much as it did the regular clergy of the Established Church. Still the great work of evangelisation progressed despite every opposition, and has continued ever since to gain strength.

The services of lay preachers in Wales are not confined to preaching-rooms and small branch congregations. They are frequently invited to occupy the pulpits of the most respectable congregations while the ministers are engaged at the out-stations or elsewhere. No minister in the Principality would hesitate to engage a pious tradesman, mechanic, or labourer, who could talk common sense in the shape of a sermon, to supply his pulpit in his absence. This good understanding between the ministers and their lay brethren produces the most salutary effects. The Churches of Wales have but seldom been troubled during the last hundred years by priestly assumptions on the part of ministers, or the wild desire to do away with a stated ministry altogether on the part of the people. The institution of lay preaching, as it exists among us, acts as a balance of power to keep both ministers and people from those opposite extremes.

Having occupied so much of your space with the foregoing remarks on preaching, I can only just mention our Sabbath-schools, with their peculiar characteristics, and our institution of cottage prayer-meetings, as important agencies, in connection with preaching, in the evangelisation of the people. The weekly labours of from thirty to forty thousand Sabbath-school teachers, and ten or fifteen thousand pious men who are going from cottage to cottage to conduct prayer-meetings, cannot fail to be attended with the most beneficial results.

The success of evangelistic work among the working classes of Wales is, in a great measure, to be attributed to the fact that the Dissenting churches have always kept clear of the imprudence, or rather the sin, of making any invidious distinction between one class and another in connection with religion. We readily recognise the usual distinction of classes in our daily intercourse and secular transactions, but the moment we cross the threshold of the sanctuary, or meet to hold a religious service anywhere, our social distinctions are entirely forgotten. The clergy of the Establishment, in many parts of the Principality, have emptied their churches by not paying due attention to this point. In several parishes, the most convenient part of the Sabbath is chosen by the rector to preach to the *élite* of the parish, while an inconveniently early or late hour is allotted to the common people to hear a sermon from the curate. Some clergymen also administer the Lord's Supper to the gentry and the lower classes at different hours. Such arrangements have driven away almost every respectable working man from those churches, leaving only mendicants to attend them for the sake of the loaves and fishes.

Separate services, free sittings, and a distinct class of teachers for the working classes, would never have succeeded to win them in Wales, and they will never succeed anywhere else. The Welsh churches do not raise their ministers' salaries by pew-rents, and therefore they can afford to let the sittings at such a moderate rate, which every working man who is not a pauper can pay, and working men always had rather pay than occupy a free sitting. Our churches do not consider a lay preacher or a town missionary qualified to stand up as a preacher anywhere if he cannot occasionally deliver an acceptable discourse from the pulpit of the minister under whose auspices he exercises his gifts elsewhere. The men sent out to teach the working classes, if not deemed worthy to appear as occasional supplies in any pulpit in the locality where they labour, are not likely to do much good to the classes to whom they are sent.

THE ALLEGED UNCHASTITY OF WALES.

A PAPER READ AT ONE OF THE SOCIAL SCIENCE MEETINGS OF THE NATIONAL EISTEDDFOD HELD AT SWANSEA, IN SEPT., 1863.

It is an unquestionable fact, strange and unaccountable as it is, that the condition of Wales and the elements of the Welsh character are but very imperfectly understood by our English neighbours. They seem to be much better acquainted with everything pertaining to the nations of the Continent than they are with the affairs of their Welsh fellow subjects. Hence their readiness to believe every incredible and ridiculous report respecting us.

About seventeen years ago the Government sent down three Commissioners to inquire into the state of Education in Wales. Unhappily these gentlemen found their way into the society of a number of hypochondriac and misanthropic Welshmen, who gave them a most gloomy and unfavourable account of the moral character of the nation. The depositions of these persons, together with the evident predetermination of the Commissioners themselves to make out a case against us, led them to present reports to Parliament containing the foulest defamation of our character as a nation. We are represented as semi-barbarians. Petty thefts, lying, cozening, every species of chicanery, drunkenness, and idleness, are said to prevail amongst us, and our women are accused of being *almost universally unchaste*. The vice of unchastity is stated to be flagrant throughout North Wales, remain unchecked by any instruments of civilization, and to have obtained for so long a time *as the peculiar vice of the Principality*, that its existence has almost ceased to be considered as an evil.

These wholesale calumniations, as might have been expected, excited at the time a considerable degree of indignation against our calumniators throughout the nation. Poets, orators, the conductors of our periodical literature, and other talented patriots, came forth as a mighty and well armed host in our defence, but among our able defenders the foremost place is due to our excellent and able countryman, Sir Thomas Phillips, and the lamented Ieuan Gwynedd, who have immortalised their names by their unanswerable replies to the calumnies of the reports. Yet, able and convincing as these replies are, it does not appear that they have succeeded in removing the false impression left on the English mind by the reports of the Commissioners. The belief still prevails to a great extent in England that the charges of the reports against us are all true.

It is not my intention in this brief paper to refer to all the charges preferred against us. I shall only notice the charge of almost universal unchastity.

It would be preposterous to deny that the sin of unchastity exists in Wales, as well as in other countries, but the sweeping assertion that it is *a vice peculiar to the Principality*, or even that it is as prevalent in Wales as it is in England, is utterly unfounded. Prostitution—the most degrading vice of corrupt humanity—is almost unknown in the Principality, except in a few of the largest seaport towns, and the most populous localities of the manufacturing districts. There are whole counties in South and North Wales in which hardly a single public prostitute can be found; and in those towns of the counties of Monmouth and Glamorgan, where this vice chiefly prevails, only a small proportion of the abandoned characters are Welsh girls. The Welsh are decidedly as free as any civilized nation on the face of the earth from unchastity under the disgusting garb of prostitution.

Conjugal infidelity is also of comparatively rare occurrence in the Principality. Many large districts of the country might be named in which not one instance of known adultery had been found during a whole generation. The sacredness

of the marriage covenant, and the enormity of the sin of
adultery, are, happily, regarded and felt throughout the
nation. Wales, in this respect, can advantageously bear
comparison with England.

The number of illegitimate children born in any district is,
of itself, by no means a correct test of the chastity or the
unchastity of the people, for it is a fact that in proportion to
the prevalence of prostitution the number of illegitimate
births diminishes. It would, therefore, be unfair and absurd
to infer from the fact that the per centage of bastards in
Wales is higher than in London and other large English towns,
that unchastity is more prevalent in the Principality than in
those sinks of uncleanness.

In the Twenty-fourth Report of the Registrar-General (and
the former reports give us similar results) we find that the
number of children born out of wedlock in the year 1861 was
rather more than six to every hundred births throughout the
whole of England and Wales, while the average for Monmouthshire and South Wales is rather less than six per cent.,
and that for North Wales above seven per cent. By compar-
ing the agricultural and the manufacturing districts of Wales
with English districts of the same description, the result is
decidedly in favour of Wales. The following table shows the
proportion of illegitimate births to every hundred births in
Wales, and those English counties whose inhabitants most
resemble those of Wales in social positions and occupations:—

The whole of England and Wales	6.3
Monmouthshire	5.6
South Wales	6.2
North Wales	7.4
Suffolk	8.1
Herefordshire	8.6
North Riding of Yorkshire	9.2
Shropshire	9.8
Nottinghamshire	9.9
Norfolk	10.3
Westmoreland	10.6
Cumberland	11.2

It will thus appear that unchastity is not a vice peculiar to
the Principality, but that under its various odious forms of
prostitution, adultery, and illegitimacy, it is much more
prevalent in England than in Wales. The Welsh are, beyond
question, in point of chastity far superior to the English; and

their unchastity, as far as it prevails, wears a much less disgusting form than the same vice in England. The illicit intercourse of young people previous to marriage—or where a solemn promise of marriage is made—the almost only form of unchastity in Wales, culpable and sinful as it is, is not for a moment to be compared in enormity with the aggravated crimes of adultery and systematic prostitution, the most prevalent forms of unchastity in English towns. Still, considering that the bulk of the middle and the lower classes in Wales are either professors of religion or regular attendants at places of religious worship, which is not the case to nearly the same extent with the corresponding classes in England, the degree to which unchastity prevails among us is painful and most disgraceful. In the year 1861 the illegitimate children born in the thirteen Welsh counties amounted to the enormous number of 2,795. To these might be added a considerable number of young women who enter the married state in an unbecoming condition. This state of things is certainly most unworthy of a people so highly privileged as the Welsh are.

The comparative prevalence of illicit intercourse between the sexes in Wales has been attributed to different causes. One of the Education Commissioners had the audacity to attribute it to a *total* want of mental cultivation and the means of moral training!! If so, how are we to account for the fact that in Scotland—the most thoroughly educated portion of the United Kingdom—the per centage of illegitimate births is one-third higher than in Wales? The disgusting revelations of the Divorce Court also prove that members of the most cultivated and highest classes of English society are incomparably more depraved than the most uneducated of the Welsh peasants. Neither should we forget the glaring fact that a large proportion of the seducers of our poor Welsh girls belong to the most cultivated class in the community. Do not these facts demonstrate that mental cultivation, however valuable it may be, is not sufficient without something superior with it, to secure moral purity?

Others have referred to the want of convenient and separate bedrooms for the different sexes in the dwellings of the working classes and the small farmers as a special cause of unchastity. It is, to say the least, most indecent for unmarried men and women to sleep in the same room, and must be anything but favourable to the cultivation of modesty and chastity. Happily, this unbecoming custom is being gradually done away with by the erection of more commodious farmhouses, and better dwellings for the poor. Yet, in spite of the unfavourable and tempting circumstances under which a large number of the Welsh peasantry are placed, the number of illegitimate births in the counties of Hereford and Salop, where convenient dwellings are provided for the lower classes, is nearly one-third higher than in the Principality. The natural inference to be drawn from this fact is that the inhabitants of Wales, under all their disadvantages, are more virtuous than their better conditioned neighbours in the adjoining English counties.

The first and the real cause of unchastity, as well as of every other sin, is the corruption of human nature, and the want of the fear of God as the governing principle of the heart; but many secondary causes might be named which may differ in different countries. The secondary causes of unchastity in Wales, and some of which may be peculiar to the Principality, appear to be :

1. *Premature Courtship.*—Children at the early age of from thirteen to fifteen often begin courting, and before finishing their education or learning any trade, they talk earnestly of getting married. Should poverty, the opposition of their parents, or other circumstances, prevent their immediate entrance into the married state, they will become a prey to their youthful lusts. The consequence will be either a bastard child, or a foolish and disgraceful marriage.

2. *Courting at improper hours and places.*—It is useless to attempt to conceal the disgraceful fact that young people almost universally throughout the agricultural districts of Wales meet stealthily in the depth of night in barns, haylofts, the kitchens of farmhouses, and even in bedrooms, to court. And this tempting and unbecoming practice is rather encouraged than checked by the middle and the lower classes. The general opinion is that decency requires courtship to be carried on with the utmost secrecy until within a few weeks of the marriage. Should a young couple venture to sit or walk together in the day time, the remark would at once be made, "See how impudent those creatures are." Considering the improper hours and places which our youth are, in a sense, compelled by public opinion to use for purposes of courtship, it is astonishing that the instances of unchastity which come to light are not ten times more numerous than they are.

3. *The use of obscene songs and immodest language.*—There

F

is not a language probably in the whole world whose literature is purer than the Welsh. We feel thankful to God that we can state that there is not a single infidel or immoral work of any note in our language; still it must be confessed that some of our poets, especially in former ages, have prostituted their talents to compose songs and verses which are not adapted to answer any purposes but to corrupt the minds of those who read and repeat them. It is true that but a few of these impure compositions have ever appeared in print, but there is hardly any district of the country in which obscene songs and stanzas are not often repeated and sung by the most dissolute of the people. The use of immodest language in common conversation is, there is reason to fear, very prevalent among our working classes. None, of course, but the most abandoned characters are in the habit of cursing and swearing, and blaspheming the name of God; while thousands, who would shudder at the idea of uttering oaths and curses, do not hesitate to use obscene language. God only knows to what extent the minds of our young people are corrupted by the immodest conversation of their seniors.

4. *The large fairs which are held in every town and village throughout the country, to which crowds of young men and women resort, have a direct tendency to corrupt their morals.* —Farmers' sons and servants in Wales seldom taste intoxicating drinks except at the fairs, three or four times a year. On these occasions some of them use it rather too freely. Detained at the fairs to a late hour by company, amusements, and other temptations, many half intoxicated young men on their return home venture to take such liberties with their female companions as their consciences and sense of propriety would not have permitted them to take at other times. The fairs have proved occassions of disgrace and ruin to thousands of our young people.

In order to remedy this evil, parents and masters, whose children or servants may be of marriageable age, should ungrudgingly grant them convenient and proper time for courting—say three or four hours weekly. They should also insist that their courtship should not be carried on clandestinely, and at improper hours and places. Young people will court whether permitted or not, and if convenient time be not granted them for it, they will meet at those hours when all honest men should be in the fond embraces of sleep. Let heads of families, the ministers of religion, and every friend of moral purity, use all their influence to put down the disgraceful and dangerous habit of night courting, and to impress upon the minds of our youth that it is the eye of the adulterer that waiteth for the twilight, while every chaste man and woman should not be ashamed to keep company with the future companion of his or her life "in the face of the sun and the eye of light." As long as the erroneous idea clings to the mind of the community, that concealed is more decent than unconcealed courtship, unchastity will continue to trouble and disgrace us, however perfect and efficient the means of our mental cultivation and religious privileges may be. Open courtship, while it would, to a considerable extent at least, check the prevalence of unchastity, would also prove an effectual barrier to many premature and unwise marriages. The whole country from Cardiff to Holyhead should be so agitated on this subject by means of the press and public meetings, as to convince every householder of his imperative duty not to tolerate nocturnal courtship on his premises, and to inspire every young man and woman with a deep sense of the disgraceful character and baneful effects of the practice.

Special efforts should also be made to impress upon the minds of the people a deeper sense of the enormity of the sin of unchastity. It must be confessed that public opinion in Wales does not stamp on this vice that infamy which it deserves. The poor seduced women with us, as well as in England, lose caste when they fall; but the *men*, their diabolical seducers, almost universally escape the curses of public opinion. It seems quite unaccountable why the community to a man should agree to shun the company of thieves and swindlers, while the ruiners of our innocent girls are freely admitted to decent society. The burglar who enters a man's house to rob him of his money, is a most venial offender in comparison with the consummate villain who robs his wife, daughter, or sister, of her virtue. It is to be feared that parents take more pains to impress the minds of their children with the importance of honesty, industry, and other virtues, than they do to teach them the importance of chastity. Unchastity is too generally regarded among us as a weakness rather than a crime of the deepest dye. The pulpit too—the most powerful instrument to affect the Welsh mind—does not denounce this sin with that power and unsparing severity with which other sins are denounced. The supposed difficulty of treating this subject with such plainness and force as to be effective, and at the same time with that delicacy which becomes the pulpit, probably deters most ministers from attempting to do more than refer to it incidentally. This is not as it should be. While the sin prevails in the community, no sense of delicacy should deter the ministers of God from lifting up their voices like trumpets to denounce it.

If the Welsh are not so deeply sunk in this sin as the surrounding nations, still we have no ground for boasting. "We are verily guilty;" the national character is stained, and nothing less than national repentence and reformation can wipe off the stain. Let us all—parents and children, ministers and people, rich and poor, old and young—humble ourselves before God; unite heart and soul to suppress every national custom that fosters impurity, and use every available means to elevate the moral sentiment of the people, so that that abhorent vice which has from age to age disgraced our religious profession, destroyed the happiness of numberless families, and blighted the prospects of thousands of our sons and daughters for time and eternity, may henceforth be not so much as named among us.

EDUCATION IN WALES.

Mr. Bowstead, Her Majesty's Inspector of Schools, having stated in his report for the years 1854—5, that unsectarian Schools were the only kind of Schools adapted for South Wales, the Bishop of St. David's, in his charge to his Clergy some years after, flatly contradicted that statement, and asserted that Nonconformists had no objection to National or Church Schools. Mr. Bowstead, by way of self-defence, addressed a circular to several Nonconformist ministers and laymen in Wales, asking for their views on the point at issue between him and the Bishop. He received 122 replies, which he printed for private circulation. The following letter is the third in that collection.

Beaufort, December 29, 1860.

Dear Sir,

I have read the remarks of the Bishop of St David's in his last Charge to the Clergy of his diocese, on your report of 1854—5 on the condition and prospects of popular education in South Wales, with a large measure of astonishment. That a person of Dr. Thirlwall's learning and reputed liberality of sentiment, should become the avowed advocate of a system of education for the working classes of his diocese which involves all the elements of sectarianism, injustice, oppression, and persecution, is certainly most surprising. His Lordship well knows, or ought to know, that full nine-tenths of the population of South Wales are Dissenters, and that of the comparatively small minority who are Churchmen, the largest proportion belong to the upper and middle classes, whose children are not educated at either National or British Schools. Enormous sums have already been granted by Government towards the establishment and support of exclusive Church Schools in South Wales, while of the children expected to attend those schools scarcely one-twentieth are the children of Churchmen. Grants to Church Schools in such a population can therefore be viewed in no other light than *grants for Church extension.* To apply for those grants under such circumstances, appears to me most unfair and underhanded. The educational grants are annually voted by the House of Commons for the *specific purpose* of educating the children of the working classes, not for advancing the interest of any church or religious denomination as such. In order, therefore, to secure portions of those grants for the support of Church Schools in most districts of South Wales, the *spirit* of the regulations by which the Committee of Council on Education distribute them must be violated, if not their *letter* also. It can hardly be consistent with those regulations to aid denominational schools in districts where scarcely a dozen children belonging to such denominations could be found; but consistent or not, such has been the case in the establishment of most National Schools in South Wales. The consequence is, that coercion, bribery, and other unfair means are used to force or induce dissenting parents to send their children to those schools.

As far as I understand the views and feelings of the Dissenters of South Wales, and it would be no presumption to say that I understand them quite as well as his Lordship, you have correctly represented them in the report upon which he animadverts. British Schools are the only schools adapted for Wales. There may be exceptions in some of the largest towns, where both Church and Dissenting Schools might prove efficient, but even there, popular education would, most certainly, be better promoted by well conducted unsectarian schools. If Churchmen have nothing more in

view in the establishment of day schools than the elevation of
the masses, by furnishing them with the means of education
on Christian principles, it is difficult to conceive what
objection they can have to join their dissenting neighbours in
establishing and supporting British Schools.   Dissenters have
insuperable objections to National Schools on account of their
exclusive and sectarian character, but what objection can be
raised by Churchmen against British Schools?   Is there a
sentence in favour of dissent and against the Established
Church in any of the publications of the British and Foreign
School Society, or any other books used in these Schools?
Where in Wales are British Schools so managed as to furnish
the most rigid Churchman with the least shadow of reason for
not supporting them?   The fact is, as long as the grants of
the Committee of Council are made to denominational Schools,
especially in the rural districts of South Wales, whether they
be church or dissenting schools, it will only be a waste of the
public money; for such schools will never prosper nor secure
the confidence of the community.   Why should not all parties
meet on the broad and unobjectionable platform of the British
and Foreign School Society?   And why should the progress
of popular education be retarded by forcing the peculiar
dogmas of sects into day schools, while we have the Sunday
schools, the pulpits, the press, and numberless other means
and opportunities for indoctrinating our people in the peculiarities of our different creeds?   If the schoolmaster is
expected to do more than furnish his pupils with correct ideas
of the fundamental truths of natural and revealed religion, the
leading facts of Scripture history, and the pure morality of the
New Testament, what is left for the Christian minister to do?
     I wonder how his Lordship ventures to contradict your
self-evident statement "that dissenting parents hold the
Catechism and other formularies of the Church in a sort of
abhorence."   What parent, with the least sense of morality,
would not abhor a kind of teaching which would lead his
child to utter a downright falsehood?   How can the children
of Dissenters repeat the Church Catechism without uttering
what is not true?   The children of the Antipœdo-Baptists
are not baptized, and the children of all other dissenting
parents have neither godfathers nor godmothers when baptized.
But there is a still more serious objection to the Church
Catechism.   As understood by all the dissenting bodies, and
even as explained by the highest authorities in the Church,

it plainly teaches the doctrine of *Baptismal Regeneration,* and that doctrine, whether true or false, is held by the Dissenters of Wales *universally* in as much abhorence as the most detestable dogmas of the Church of Rome.   Until his Lordship therefore can disprove these facts, your statement will stand for an undeniable truth and not an "absurd exaggeration." To say that many dissenting parents send their children to the National Schools proves nothing more than that many working men are compelled to do so by unfair means; that several poor parents are tempted by the charities placed at the. disposal of the Clergy to betray their principles; that many having no other school in their neighbouohood to which they can send their children, send them to the National School, trusting to the influence of home instruction, the Sunday schools, and the dissenting ministry, to counteract what they deem erroneous in the religious teaching of the day school; and that the Managers of National Schools in those localities where they have to compete with British Schools generally dispense with everything objectionable to Dissenters.

The Dissenters of Wales cannot help looking upon the present extraordinary zeal of Churchmen to educate the people, with a considerable degree of suspicion, for two reasons: 1. They are scarcely anywhere willing to co-operate with them in the support of schools, on purely unsectarian principles, in which all parties might have confidence.   2. This zeal of theirs is something of a very modern date.   In former ages, Churchmen, with a few honourable exceptions, were mortally opposed to the education of the people.   Let the following facts serve as proofs of this statement: of ten editions of the sacred Scriptures published in the Welsh language from 1641 to 1690, only one folio edition for the parish churches was published by Churchmen.   Thomas Gouge and Stephen Hughes, in the latter part of the seventeenth century, were most barbarously persecuted by the Clergy and gentry for their self-denying efforts to establish schools, and disseminate the word of God in the Principality.   The apostolic Griffith Jones, Vicar of Llanddowror, in the eighteenth century, had to encounter the most virulent opposition from the Bishops and the generality of the Clergy, in his laudable endeavours to establish Welsh circulating schools; and even a bishop employed an unprincipled clergyman to defame him in one of the most scurrilous and vulgar pamphlets ever issued by the British press, and that for no other crime than his disinterested efforts to educate his benighted countrymen; for which same offence he was harassed for nearly twenty years in the Ecclesiastical Court. If this account should appear to his Lordship of St. David's as an "absurd exaggeration," he will find it is not so, if he will take the trouble of searching the records of his own court from 1730 to 1750. The labours of Mr. Charles, of Bala, and Dr. Edward Williams, of Oswestry, at a later period of the same century, were not better encouraged. I merely mention these facts to show that Dissenters have grounds to suspect that the present zeal of Churchmen to promote education does not arise from a simple desire to instruct the people. If, differing from their forefathers, they sincerely aim to elevate the people by promoting popular education, why do they refuse to join their dissenting brethren on neutral grounds, which would be the only way to do the. work efficiently?

Government grants to any amount for the support of National Schools will never promote popular education in Wales, nor even secure the object, which many Churchmen have evidently in view in establishing Church Schools—the crushing of Dissent. If they can ever attain that object, they must attain it, not by means of day schools, but by excelling dissenting ministers in piety, ministerial efficiency, and Christian charity. Should they ever secure what they aim at by those means, heaven and earth will rejoice in their success.

Expecting that you will triumphantly vindicate yourself and the cause of popular unsectarian education in Wales against his Lordship's imbecile attack,

I am, &c.,

THOMAS REES.

WELSH LITERATURE.

A LECTURE DELIVERED AT THE ROYAL INSTITUTION OF SOUTH WALES, SWANSEA, FEBRUARY THE 18TH, 1867.

IT is not probable that any living language, understood and spoken by less than a million of people, has such a vast store of literature as the Welsh.

Immense quantities of Welsh MSS. have been transmitted from the middle ages, and are still preserved at the British Museum, and other public and private libraries, consisting of poetry, statutes, national proverbs, triads, histories, legends, and superstitious fables. Those who wish to have a full account of these remains of ancient lore, may find it in the Myvyrian Archaiology, the publications of the Welsh MSS. Society, and Stephens' Literature of the Kymry. The fact that such a number of the literary productions of the tenth, and the five following centuries, should have escaped the ravages of time, and the incessant wars in which the Welsh nation were engaged during those centuries, demonstrates that our forefathers, considering the almost universal ignorance which characterised their times, were an eminently learned people, and not such rude uncultivated barbarians as they have too often been represented by prejudiced historians.

At the very dawn of the Protestant Reformation, in the sixteenth century, the light of a superior kind of knowledge to that cultivated in the dark ages, began to shine in Wales, and it has ever since continued to scatter its rays with increasing splendour year after year, until the whole land is now so filled with the means of useful knowledge, that no monoglott Welshman can find any valid excuse for being ignorant.

In the year 1717, the Rev. Moses Williams, Vicar of Devynock, Breconshire, published a catalogue of as many printed Welsh books as were then in existence, or as many of them as had come under his notice, with interesting notices of several of their authors, translators, or publishers. That valuable list was incomplete; but the industrious author in his preface promises a supplement or a new edition of his work at some future time. That promise was never fulfilled, probably owing to the removal of the author to Bridgewater, in England, where he died in the year 1742. In 1840 a new list, embodying the whole of Williams' list, with numerous additions and a continuation to the close of the eighteenth century, was published in the *Gwladgarwr*, a Welsh periodical. That list contains the titles of six hundred and twenty Welsh books, including a few English and Latin works on subjects relating to Wales, printed from the year 1531 to 1799. A still more complete catalogue, prepared by the late Rev. William Rowlands, a Wesleyan Methodist minister, appeared in the *Traethodydd*, another Welsh periodical, in the

G

years 1852 and 1853. This list contains the names of no less
than thirteen hundred and fifty books issued by· the Welsh
press from 1531 to 1799. Full as this catalogue was, the
careful and painstaking compiler soon found that it was far
from being a complete list of all the Welsh publications issued
during that period. He continued to the close of his industrious life to find out books not included in his printed· list,
and carefully copied their titles. His revised and greatly
extended catalogue, containing matter enough to fill a large
closely printed octavo volume, was nearly ready for the press
when death put a period to his useful and patriotic labours.
It is expected that his manuscript will soon be published
under the superintendence of a competent editor.

The number of books printed in the Welsh language,
including repeated editions of the productions of a few
popular authors, from the middle of the sixteenth to the close
of the eighteenth century, amounts to nearly two thousand
distinct works; but large as this number is, it is very
insignificant when compared with the number published
since the commencement of the present century. The rapid
extension of trade, the increase of the population, and the
establishment of Sunday and day schools through the length
and breadth of the Principality within the last seventy years,
have created an unprecedented demand for books, and the
supply has been fully equal to the demand. No attempt has
been made to compile a catalogue of all the Welsh publications
of the last sixty-six years; but it would be no exaggeration
to say that their number, reckoning every production from the
folio family Bible to the penny pamphlet, exceeds eight
thousand.

· The first printed book in the Welsh language was published
in 1531. It was a kind of a school book, entitled *Primer*,
and consisted of twenty-one leaves. The author was one of
the Salesburies—a name which figures conspicuously ·in the
annals of early Welsh literature, and the printer was Robert
Copeland, a person who had been in the service of William
Caxton, the first English printer. In 1535 another book,
entitled *Salesbury's Primer*, was published, which was probably a second edition of the first Primer. After the lapse of
eleven years, a third Welsh book made its appearance in 1546.
It bore the high-sounding title, *The Bible*. It was only a
small pamphlet containing the Welsh alphabet, a calendar, a
translation of the ten commandments, the Lord's prayer, and

the apostles' creed, with some remarks on what was called The seven virtues of the Church, probably the seven sacraments of the Church of Rome; and something concerning the national games of the Welsh. Sir John Price, of Brecon, is the reputed author of this book. In 1547 an English-Welsh Dictionary, compiled by William Salesbury, the celebrated translator of the New Testament, was published; and in the following year a second edition of the same work appeared. In 1550, Salesbury published "A brief and plain introduction, teaching how to pronounce the letters in the British Tongue," together with an octavo volume entitled, "*Dymchweliad allor uchel y Pab,*" i.e., "The overthrow of the Pope's high altar." The industrious Salesbury again in 1551 published a third edition of his Dictionary, and a translation of the Psalms, the Gospels, and the Epistles, as read in the Churches at the celebration of the communion, and on Sundays and fast days.

From 1551 to 1565 no additional Welsh book was published. The death of King Edward, the accession of Queen Mary, the re-establishment of Roman Catholicism, and the persecutions, which followed, together with the national commotions connected with the repeated ecclesiastical and political changes of the times, may partly account for this inactivity of the Welsh press for so many years; but the chief cause evidently was, that adequate encouragement was not rendered to the cultivators of our national literature in the prosecution of their patriotic, but difficult and expensive work. The leading men of those times, in both Church and State, would have preferred seeing the Welsh language die away, rather than do anything to perpetuate it. It was the general impression then in England that the Welsh would never become loyal to the English throne, until they would give up their own language, and adopt that of their conquerors. No impression has been more groundless, as our history for the last three centuries testifies.

In 1565 a translation of the Litany was published. But the year 1567 is the most memorable in the early history of Welsh literature. Three works of national importance were carried through the press in that year—the New Testament, the Book of Common Prayer, and a Grammar of the Welsh language. William Salesbury, assisted by Bishop Richard Davies, and the Rev. Thomas Huet, was the translator of both the New Testament and the Prayer Book. Dr. Griffith

Roberts, a Physician, and a Roman Catholic in religion, was the author of the Grammar, and his work was printed at Milan, in Italy.

The period from 1567 to 1588 forms another wide gap in the annals of our literature. During these twenty-one years only two small works on practical theology, a second edition of the Prayer Book, and an Essay on Rhetoric, by W. Salesbury, were the· productions of the Welsh press; but the publication of a complete edition of the whole Bible in the Welsh language in 1588, makes ample amends for the barrenness of the previous twenty-one years. The translator and publisher of this first edition of the Welsh Bible, was Dr. Wm. Morgan, Vicar of Llanrhaiadr yn Mochnant, and afterwards successively bishop of Llandaff and St. Asaph. Dr. Morgan's translation has been pronounced by competent judges to be remarkable for its elegance, perspicuity, idiomatic purity, and above all, as a faithful version of the original languages of the sacred Scriptures. This translation, with some unimportant alterations by Bishop Parry, has been the basis of all subsequent editions of the Welsh Bible.

The total number of Welsh books, including different editions of the same works, published from the year 1531 to the end of the sixteenth century, was twenty-three. These works consisted of the Bible, or portions of it, the Prayer Book, Primers, Dictionaries, Grammars, and works on doctrinal and practical divinity. If the number of the works was but small, they were all useful books, and adapted to the wants of the nation. No worthless literary trash is named among them. Of the twenty-three Welsh books and editions published in the sixteenth century, no less than thirteen, probably more, were written or published by the Salesburies, the originators and principal cultivators of early Welsh literature. These patriotic and learned men were members of a respectable Denbighshire family. William Salesbury, the translator of the New Testament and the Prayer Book, and author of the English-Welsh Dictionary, and several other works, was the second son of Foulk Salesbury, Esquire, of Plasisaf, Llanrwst. He was born early in the sixteenth century, and was educated at Oxford. He had studied for the legal profession, but it does not appear that he ever did anything in his profession, having devoted his life to literary pursuits. He was a zealous protestant, and was exposed to imminent dangers during the reign of Queen Mary. William

Salesbury was one of the most learned men of the age. Henry Perry, the editor of his posthumous work on Rhetoric, says that he was master of nine languages besides Welsh and English, viz.:—The Hebrew, Chaldee, Syriac, Arabic, Greek, Latin, French, Italian, and Spanish. The time and place of his death are unknown.

Henry Salesbury was born at Dolbelider, in Denbighshire, in 1561. He received his University education at Oxford, where he studied for the medical profession, which he afterwards practised at Denbigh. In 1593 he published a Welsh Grammar, and left in manuscript a Welsh and Latin Dictionary, which was never published.

John Salesbury, Bishop of Sodor and Man, who died in 1573, is mentioned as a promoter of Welsh literature; but I have not been able to find out that he was the author of any Welsh book. ●

Thomas Salesbury was a Welsh poet and critic, who flourished from about 1580 to 1620. It appears that he was a London publisher. In 1603 he published Captain Middleton's metrical version of the Psalms. He also was the publisher of H. Salesbury's Grammar. One John Salesbury was a London printer, who began on the 10th of May, 1644, to issue a Whig Newspaper entitled, *The Flying Post*. Dutton, one of his contemporaries, and possibly his political opponent, gives him the strange title of *a desperate Hypergergonic Welshman*. Sir John Salesbury is also mentioned as a liberal contributor towards the expense of printing Welsh books. Salesbury is a name which will live in the affections of Welshmen as long as the Scriptures are read in the Welsh language.

It would be impracticable within the limits of a lecture to name, much less to describe, one out of every hundred of the issues of the Welsh press from the beginning of the seventeenth century to the present time. To give a short account of the general character of our literature is all I can attempt at present. We have no standard scientific works in the Welsh language, and they have never been considered necessary, as every Welshman who wishes to acquire a correct professional knowledge of the arts and sciences, is presumed to be acquainted with the English and other languages. While our literature supplies common readers with a few manuals and popular essays on almost every conceivable branch of general knowledge, the great bulk of our books are confined to divinity, history, poetry, and Welsh philology.

Our Grammars and Dictionaries are numerous. Dr. Owen Pugh's Welsh-English Dictionary is without a rival in the annals of lexicography. The first edition, which was published in 1793—1803, in two quarto volumes, contains above one hundred thousand words, with twelve thousand quotations from standard Welsh authors, ancient and modern. The second edition, published in 1832, in two royal octavo volumes, contains many thousands more words than the first. The English-Welsh Dictionaries of the Rev. D. Sylvan Evans, and the Rev. D. Hughes, B.A., also deserve to be respectfully mentioned as lasting monuments of the industry, judgment, and learning of their able compilers. They contain Welsh words for every word in the latest editions of Webster's, and other modern English Dictionaries.

Of original poetry we have scores of volumes, and hundreds of pamphlets of different sizes, besides translations of the principal works of Milton, Gray, and other celebrated English poets. Not being a poet myself, I am not competent to pronounce a judgment on the merits or demerits of the compositions of our hosts of poets, but it must be apparent to every ordinary reader that a vast deal of soulless rhymes have been published, under the name of poetry, which no one but their imbecile composers would ever have deemed worthy of any place but the fire; yet this remark is quite applicable to the poetry of other nations as to that of the Welsh. On the other hand, it is unquestionable that there are such gems to be met with, in our poetical literature, which can advantageously bear to be compared with the sublimest compositions of the best poets of any nation.

Welsh readers are tolerably well-furnished with historical works, such as a history of the World; history of Great Britain; three or four histories of Wales; three Ecclesiastical histories; history of religion in Wales; history of the Martyrs; histories of the Welsh Baptists, Methodists, and Independents; history of the Jews; and several smaller works on the history of different nations, localities, and events.

But of all subjects no one has been so thoroughly discussed and illustrated in the literature of Wales as *theology*. Books on every conceivable point of doctrinal, practical, devotional, and controversial theology are accessible to monoglott Welsh readers. There are in the Welsh language *nine* commentaries on the whole Bible, exclusive of several family Bibles, with practical and devotional notes, for family reading; nine on the

New Testament separately; several on particular books of the Bible, with a large number of works on Oriental customs, Biblical antiquities, natural history, and geography. We have eight Biblical and theological Dictionaries; seven or eight systems of theology, and works without number on practical and devotional subjects. Our works on controversial subjects are by far too numerous. Volumes and hundreds of pamphlets have been published from time to time on the points at issue between Churchmen and Dissenters; Trinitarians and Unitarians; Pædio Baptists and Anti-pædio Baptists; Calvinists and Arminians; and upon almost every nice distinction which divides one religious party from another. Some of our controversial works are most ably written; but our controversies have seldom been carried on in a spirit worthy of the professed followers of the Prince of peace.

Our periodical literature demands a brief notice. Four attempts were made in the eighteenth century to establish periodical literature in the Welsh language, and they all failed for want of support. The Rev. Josiah Rees, of Gellionen, in this county, started a fortnightly magazine, on the 3rd of March, 1770, and the last number appeared on the 15th of September, in the same year. The Rev. Morgan John Rees, of Pontypool, an able Baptist minister, published five numbers of a quarterly magazine in 1793-4, which, like its predecessor, had to be discontinued. A third unsuccessful attempt was made in 1796, by the Rev. David Davies, Independent minister at Holywell, Flintshire. The Rev. Thomas Charles, *of Bala, was the fourth to make the experiment, and he was somewhat more successful than the others, for his periodical prolonged its existence for more than two years. The Welsh Wesleyans, the youngest and the weakest religious body then in Wales, were the first party that succeeded in establishing a permanent monthly magazine. Their *Eurgrawn Wesleyaidd* was started in 1809, and has been published regularly every month ever since. The Rev. Joseph Harries, of Swansea, assisted by a few friends, commenced the publication of a weekly newspaper entitled *Seren Gomer*, January 1, 1814. It came out weekly until September 9, 1815, when, for want of adequate support, it had to be discontinued. January 1, 1818, Mr. Harries commenced publishing his *Seren Gomer* again in the form of a monthly unsectarian magazine, and his second attempt proved more successful than the first. That periodical soon became a power in Wales, and was for nearly twenty years regarded as the national magazine. Every religious body in the Principality has long since established its periodicals. At the present time *twenty-nine* monthly and quarterly magazines in the Welsh language are in circulation. There are also eight weekly papers published, and the aggregate circulation of the magazines and papers amount to 120,000.

There are several important serials now in course of publication. Seventy numbers of a Welsh Encyclopedia, to be completed in twelve large volumes, are already issued; a superb Family Bible, with extensive comments, from the press of Fullarton & Co., and a costly edition of a translation of ".Goldsmith's Animated Nature," published by the same house, are also coming out. To these might be added a Gazetteer, two Biographical Dictionaries, a complete edition of the prose and poetical works of Williams of Pantycelyn, &c., &c. Some people prophesy the extinction of the Welsh language in a short time. Whether that prophecy will be fulfilled or not, one thing is certain, that the Welsh press has never been so active as it is at present. There are more books published now in one year than there were in ten years fifty years ago.

The circulation of Welsh books is necessarily limited. It is calculated that not above eight hundred and fifty thousand, or two-thirds of the inhabitants of the Principality, understand the Welsh language; and of that number nearly one-half understand the English as well as the Welsh, and most of those, for various reasons, prefer and confine themselves to English literature. Welsh books and newspapers are chiefly circulated among not above half a million of people, mostly of the poorer classes in the community. Notwithstanding the comparatively small number of our monoglott Welsh population, they are supplied with enormous quantities of books. The British and Foreign Bible Society has sold seventy thousand copies of the Scriptures in Wales and Monmouthshire last year, and that Society since its formation in 1804, has circulated upwards of a million of copies. Large numbers of the Bibles issued by the Society for promoting Christian Knowledge are also annually circulated in Wales, and within the last sixty years above twenty editions of Welsh Family Bibles with·Notes have been issued by Welsh, English, and Scotch publishers. Where, except in Wales, is to be found a community of half a million of people, consisting of artizans, miners, small farmers, and agricultural labourers, among whom such numbers of books are circulated?

Welsh literature is remarkable for its religious character and high moral tone. The bulk of our books, as I have already noticed, are on religious subjects, and those works which professedly treat secular subjects, are all written in a religious spirit. We have no infidel or irreligious books within the whole compass of our literature, and were it not for the bitterness with which our controversies are too often carried on, the productions of the Welsh press would be everything which the most devout mind could wish them to be. Works of an immoral tendency, with the exception of a few ballads, and the compositions of a small number of disreputable characters among our poets, chiefly of past ages, have not found their way into our literature. Novels, the disgrace of English literature, and the curse of multitudes of English readers, do not take with Welsh readers. Our hard working men find that life is a sober reality and not a fiction, and they prefer feeding their minds with substantial truths rather than with the empty creations of the brains of novel writers.

There is one defect connected with Welsh literature which every Welshman should regret and endeavour to supply—the want of a national library, containing a copy of every Welsh book ever printed, every work in the English, and other languages, on subjects relating to Wales, and a complete collection of all the Welsh MSS. which are now scattered here and there throughout the country, and inaccessible to those who would wish to consult them for literary purposes. Hundreds of MSS. and old printed books, will in a short time be irrecoverably lost, if not deposited in a carefully kept public library. It is astonishing why some zealous and patriotic literary Welshman, should not have moved the whole nation on this important subject long ago. The establishment of a national library, is quite practicable. If three or four gentlemen of influence were to move in the matter, the object might be easily attained. What an honour such an Institution would be to the Welsh nation, and what a boon to antiquarians, literary inquirers, and the public at large? No nation in Europe, except the Welsh, possessing such a store of literary treasures, is destitute of public libraries, where the writings of its learned men are deposited and kept with scrupulous care. How long will our nation, contenting itself with mere empty adulations of its great men in grandiloquent orations at the *Eisteddfodau,* leave the precious productions of their powerful

and active minds, to rot in damp rooms or thrown into the
fire as waste papers? Cartloads of valuable manuscripts and
old books have been thus destroyed in Wales within the last
fifty years.

As Swansea has for centuries occupied a very prominent
place in the annals of Welsh literature, a short account of
what has been done here, from time to time, to promote its
cultivation, may not be deemed inappropriate at the close
of this lecture.   In the seventeenth century the Rev.
Stephen Hughes, an eminent Nonconformist minister, who
resided in this town for the last twenty-six years of his life,
and whose mortal remains rest in St. John's Churchyard,
published upwards of twenty Welsh books.   The Rev. David
Jones, another learned Nonconformist minister, who resided
here for some years, published in 1690 an edition of ten
thousand copies of the Welsh Bible.   He also published
several other Welsh books.   The Rev. David Davies, minister
of Ebenezer Chapel, who died in 1816, was about completing
the publication of a splendid edition of the Bible, with
explanatory notes, when called to his reward.   Early in the
present century, as we have already seen, the Rev. Joseph
Harries started here the first Newspaper ever printed in the
Welsh language, and afterwards for years edited and published an able and influential monthly Magazine.   Mr.
Harries, probably, did more than any of his contemporaries to
make Welsh literature a power in the community.   Neither
should we omit to mention the name of one of our living
fellow-townsmen, the Rev. Evan Griffiths, of High-street.
No living Welshman has done more than our respected friend
to supply his countrymen with the means of religious and
general knowledge.   He has accomplished the herculean task
of translating, printing, and publishing, the voluminous Com-
mentary of Matthew Henry on the Bible—a task sufficiently
heavy to paralize the energies of any man of ordinary courage
and application.*   After completing that great work, Mr.

* Two unsuccessful attempts to accomplish this task had been made
previously to his undertaking it.   The first at Dolgelley, North Wales;
but after the Pentateuch was carried through the press, the publisher
failed.   After the lapse of about three years it was resumed by a publisher
at Swansea (Mr. Harries's successor); but, unfortunately, after publishing
a few numbers, he also failed.   At that time, Mr. G., who had been
engaged in translating it, was urged to take the whole charge upon

Griffiths' busy pen could not rest. He has since published a convenient Welsh-English Dictionay, a collection of Welsh Hymns; and translated Burder's Oriental Customs; Doddridge's Rise and Progress, Brooks' Mute Christian, James' Church Member's Guide, Finney's Lectures on Revivals of Religion, Finney's Sermons, and published from twenty to thirty smaller works, some of which are translations, but the majority are original compositions, and among them there is an admirable compendium of the Ecclesiastical history of England and Wales for the last three centuries, in the catechetical form. The name of Evan Griffiths, of Swansea, is destined to live as long as the Welsh language.

Since the inhabitants of Swansea have, from age to age, taken such a prominent part in the cultivation of Welsh, literature, would it be too much to expect a few of them again to unite, in one determined effort, to enlarge and improve the library of the Royal Institution of South Wales, and make its collection of Welsh books and manuscripts so complete, that it may with propriety be denominated THE WELSH NATIONAL LIBRARY?

THE CHURCH ESTABLISHMENT IN WALES IN RELATION TO THE WELSH PEOPLE.

A PAPER READ AT THE CONFERENCE OF THE LIBERATION SOCIETY, HELD AT SWANSEA, SEPTEMBER 23, 1863.

THE ESTABLISHED CHURCH NEVER THE CHURCH OF THE PEOPLE.

IF, by a National Church, we are to understand a religious Establishment which the bulk of a nation would look upon as their sole and authoritative guide in spiritual matters, the Welsh people have not, and never had, a National Church

---

himself. It was with great reluctance he did so, knowing that the public, by this time, had but little confidence it could ever be completed. However, by perseverance and indefatigable exertion, he had the great happiness of completing it. The first parts had to be reprinted.

since the overthrow of Roman Catholicism in the reign of Henry VIII. There was no nation in Europe more attached to the Church of Rome in the beginning of the sixteenth century than the Welsh, and the ecclesiastical changes forced upon them by their Sovereigns and their Parliaments in the reigns of Henry VIII., Edward VI., and Elizabeth, were nothing more than mere political revolutions: the religious element had hardly anything to do with them, save only in name. The Welsh Clergy of that age, among whom there was a small number of earnest Papists, and a still smaller number of half-hearted Protestants, were, as a body, an un-principled class of men, who cared for nothing but their livings. Hence we find them, during that eventful period from 1534 to 1558, turning to and fro from Popery to Protestantism and from Protestantism to Popery without the least apparent scruple of conscience; and those few among them who were Protestants, were not men of such brilliancy of talent, energy of character, and ardent piety, as to deserve to be classed with the least eminent of the English, Scotch, or continental Reformers of the sixteenth century. The sudden enforcement of a new form of religion upon a Popish nation by Acts of Parliament, when no able and energetic teachers of that religion arose in the nation itself, soon effected what might have been expected—a transition from superstition to irreligion. In the preamble of an Act of Parliament passed in the fifth year of the reign of Queen Elizabeth, we are informed that "her Majesty's most loving and obedient subjects, inhabiting within her Highness's dominion and Country of Wales, are utterly destitute of God's Holy Word, and do remain in the like, or *rather more*, darkness and ignorance than they were in the time of Papistry." Notwithstanding, however, the spiritual destitution of the people, no edition of the Welsh Bible made its appearance till after the lapse of twenty-five years from the date of this Act. The edition then published was a huge folio, intended exclusively for the pulpit of the parish churches. A second folio edition, for the same purpose, was published thirty-two years after the first. It does not appear that any efforts were made during the whole of this period to provide copies of the Word of God for the use of families; and only a few persecuted Puritans attempted to preach it effectively in the churches. Those earnest ministers were expelled from the pulpits of the Establishment in the year 1633, and the following years, for refusing to read the

"Book of Sports." They soon after began to traverse the country as Nonconforming preachers, and, as might be supposed, found the people as deeply sunk in ignorance, and more irreligious, when a nominally Protestant and well-paid hierarchy was set up as their spiritual instructress, than they were a hundred years before.

We are often told that the Welsh people have been seduced from the Church by Dissenting teachers. That cannot be true; for they never were found in the churches. The Nonconformists of the seventeenth, the Methodists of the eighteenth, and the Dissenting teachers of the present century, gathered the masses to their folds, not from the parish churches, but from wakes, taverns, Sunday sports, and other irreligious amusements. The glaring failure of the Established Church to evangelise the nation, during a whole century when she had the country entirely to herself, without a single Nonconforming teacher to attract the people from her clergy, naturally leads us to conclude that Wales in the present day would have been as dark as the most unenlightened districts of Ireland, had not Protestant Nonconformity done for it what the Establishment was either unable or unadapted to accomplish. The laudable efforts of a few clergymen in former ages, and several in the present age, to promote religion and education among the middle and lower classes, have often been adduced as proofs of the utility and adaptation of the Established Church to do good. But does not the fact that she had been almost utterly useless and inactive during the first century of her existence, and comparatively so during the second, amount to a presumptive proof that she would have been to this day as useless as ever, had she not been compelled, by the activity of rival Nonconforming sects, to do something to save herself from utter extinction? The Established Church of this country, for aught we know, is as well adapted to answer the purposes of a religious establishment as that of any other country; but where is there, or has there been, a Protestant State-Church which has effected any extensive permanent good in any nation, where no Dissenting sect existed to goad her to activity?

RECENT ACTIVITY OF THE CHURCH.—RISE OF NONCONFORMITY.

As a further proof that the present life and activity of the Church are to be attributed to the existence and influence of Dissent, we may refer to the fact that the parish churches are much better attended in those districts where Dissent is most prevalent, than they are in the localities where Dissent is too feeble to exert any influence on the population. We are not able to multiply instances to illustrate this fact, as those districts in Wales where Dissent is unpopular are very few. The following instance may be sufficient to establish it. In the district of Newcastle Emlyn, where the mass of the people attend Dissenting chapels, we find that ten per cent. of the population were present at the services of the parish churches on the morning of the Census Sunday, March 30th, 1851, while on the same morning, in the district of Rhayader, Radnorshire, where the Dissenting congregations are few and small, the attendance at the parish churches was less than six per cent. of the population. We leave this fact to speak for itself.

Dissent originated and progressed in the Principality under the most unfavourable and adverse circumstances. Its founders in the seventeenth century, and its leading supporters in succeeding ages, have, from time to time, been subjected to untold obloquies, spoliations, incarcerations, and personal abuse. Yet, under the bitterest frowns of the Government, the upper classes, and an ignorant and irreligious populace, generally incited to acts of violence by persecuting clergymen, they clung to their principles with the firmness of martyrs, and propagated them throughout every nook and corner of the land with apostolic zeal. Their labours were ultimately crowned with success. The thick darkness which once covered the people gave way before the light of the Gospel of Christ; the land was filled with commodious houses of prayer, and the means of religious knowledge were made accessible to every individual throughout the whole nation. Early in the present century, when Dissent had gained such strength as to become a felt power in the Principality, the friends of the Establishment began to bestir themselves in order to prevent the ingathering of the whole nation to the fold of Nonconformity. Within the last fifty years some hundreds of churches have been erected, and a large number of Church schools established throughout the country. The Church has certainly gained a vast deal of ground since the commencement of this century; but very little in proportion to the increase of the population, and still less in proportion to the growth of Dissent, which, during the same period, has more than quintupled its places of worship, members, influence, and social respectability.

The present position of the Church and the Dissenting sects in the Principality, as far as we have been able to ascertain it, is as follows. The Church has about 1,150 places of worship, with sittings for 26 per cent. of the population; but as many of the old parish churches are situated in remote and thinly-populated districts, they are comparatively useless. The accommodation provided by the Church in the large towns and populous manufacturing districts is less than sufficient for 20 per cent. of the population, and in some localities it is much below that proportion. For instance, in the district of Neath the Establishment has accommodation for no more than 13 per cent. of the population, and in the district of Merthyr Tydvil, including Aberdare, for no more than 6 per cent.

It is impossible to ascertain with perfect accuracy what proportion of those who attend places of worship in Wales belong to the Establishment. According to the census of religious worship taken on Sunday, March, 30, 1851, we find that the aggregate number of attendants at all the places of worship in the Principality, including Monmouthshire, amounted to 968,505, and that out of that number, 174,947, or little more than one-sixth of the whole, attended the service of the Church at one part or other of the day. But from the number of attendants at the service of the Church we should deduct at least 25 per cent. for Dissenting children attending Church schools on week days, together with many of the domestics and dependants of the gentry, who, though professed Dissenters, are compelled to attend the Church occasionally. This was particularly the case on the Census Sunday, when, as is well known, special efforts were made to muster a larger attendance than usual. The proportion of Churchmen to Dissenters throughout the Principality may be put down as one to eight, but in many of the rural and manufacturing districts the preponderance of Dissenters is much greater. The total number of Dissenting places of worship is about 3,000. There may be a dozen less, or as many more. These places furnish accommodation for 60 per cent. of the population. As

---

* These statistics are for the Welsh counties proper only, and are based on Table C of the Census. The statistics usually quoted for Wales include several parishes in England, which are situated in Welsh Registration Districts. Hence the error of the writers who have attached these figures.

no more than 58 per cent. of a population can, it is calculated, attend places of worship at the same hour, the Voluntary Churches of Wales have thus supplied the deficiency of the Established Church, by providing ample accommodation, at their own expense, for every man, woman, and child, from Cardiff to Holyhead.

REVENUES OF THE ESTABLISHED CHURCH.

The almost entire failure of the Established Church to answer the professed purpose of her existence in Wales, is now a universally acknowledged fact, though different parties may not agree respecting the cause or causes of this failure. The opposition of the upper classes is not the cause, as has often been the case in Ireland. There, a large number of the gentry, as well as the populace, are staunch Catholics, and the determined opponents of Protestantism, under every name ; but the gentry of Wales, almost without exception, have, in every age, been the firm and zealous supporters of the Established Church. Neither is this failure to be attributed to the want of adequate pecuniary support, considering that the expense of living in Wales is at least twenty per cent. less than it is in England, the funds available for the support of the ministry and the various auxiliary institutions of the Church are, and have always been, comparatively enormous. The following statement, derived from various documents, such as the reports of the Ecclesiastical and Charity Commissions and the Committee of Privy Council on Education, the " Clergy List " and Parliamentary papers, will furnish a tolerably correct idea of the sums annually expended on the Establishment in Wales :—

Incomes of the four bishops	£17,100
Deans and canons	10,000
1,050 parochial benefices, averaging £220 each	231,000
Charities under the management of the clergy for the support of schools, &c..............................	23,931
Annual grants from the Committee of Council on Education to Church schools, about	10,000
Church rates and voluntary contributions in aid of Church-rates, according to parliamentary paper, No. 4, 1859	24,648
Burial and other fees, value of glebe houses, salaries of the archdeacons, chaplains in the prisons, union workhouses, &c., may be estimated at	21,000
Total..	£337,679

If to these sums be added the voluntary contributions raised towards the erection of churches, the support of schools, and various other Church institutions, the grand total would not be found much, if any, under four hundred thousand pounds a-year.

REASONS FOR THE CHURCH'S FAILURE.

The foregoing statement, it is presumed, is sufficient to convince every unprejudiced mind that had money the power to make converts to a religious party, the Welsh people would have been long since a nation of devout and zealous Churchmen. Different classes of Churchmen assign different reasons for the non-success of the Establishment in Wales. One class asserts that the entire exclusion of native Welshmen from the Episcopate, for the last hundred an fifty years, is the chief cause of the unpopularity of the Church among the Welsh people. The advocates of this opinion have taxed their imagination and their descriptive powers to the utmost in describing days of uncommon prosperity, which the Church enjoyed when the episcopal chairs were filled by Welshmen, but we have not been able to find that the Church was in any degree more prosperous then than since. The following fact does not speak very highly in favour of Welsh bishops. Dr. William Hughes, Bishop of St. Asaph, was accused, in the year 1587, of misgoverning his diocese, and of tolerating the most disgraceful abuses. When the case was inquired into, it was found that the bishop himself held sixteen rich livings *in commendam;* that most of the great livings were in the possession of persons who lived out of the country; that one person who held two of the greatest livings in the diocese, boarded in an alehouse, and that only three clergymen in the whole diocese resided upon their livings. It is hardly credible that any English prelate ever treated a Welsh diocese worse than this Welshman did. The period from 1640 to 1690 forms a considerable portion of the days of Welsh bishops. In that half century Churchmen published only one edition of the Word of God in the Welsh language—a large folio of 1,000 copies for the pulpits of the churches; while, during the same period, the persecuted and plundered Nonconformists published nine editions, consisting of about 30,000 copies of the whole Bible, and above 40,000 copies of the New Testament separately. From these facts we infer that it matters little whether the bishops be Welshmen or Englishmen. The

I

Establishment has proved equally useless to the people of Wales under prelates of both nations.

The abuse of patronage, which in every age has been most disgraceful, is given as another reason for the low state of the Establishment in Wales, while the expulsion of the Nonconformists and the Methodists from its pulpits, in the seventeenth and eighteenth centuries, is considered by some of the Evangelical clergy as the chief cause of it. We freely admit that these, and other things which might be named, may be considered as secondary causes; but the grand cause evidently is, the *unadaptedness of State Churches to convert people to real and earnest Christianity.*

PRESENT POSITION OF THE QUESTION.

Far be it from us to deny that there have been, and that there still are, a number of earnest, pious, and able ministers of the Gospel among the Welsh clergy; but the successful labours of such ministers have, almost invariably, proved more beneficial to the interests of Dissent than to those of their own church. For a proof of this assertion we need only refer to the cases of the vicars of Llandovery and Llanddowror in the seventeenth and eighteenth centuries, whose numerous converts, immediately after the deaths of the vicars, joined Dissenting churches. What the celebrated John Berridge, vicar of Everton, says in a letter to the Countess of Huntingdon, may partly account for this:—"But you say," he remarks, "the Lord is sending many Gospel labourers into the Church. True, with a view, I think, of calling his people out of it. Because when such ministers are removed by death, or transported to another vineyard, I see no fresh Gospel labourer succeed them, which obliges the forsaken flocks to fly to a meeting. And what else can they? If they have tasted of manna, and hunger for it, they cannot feed on heathen chaff, nor yet on legal crusts, though backed by some starch Pharisee quite up to perfection." However startling the sentiment may be to some people, it is unquestionably true, that whatever tends to enlighten and make people earnestly pious, tends also to weaken and destroy the influence of State Churches, which are upheld by worldly policies and compromises. It is acknowledged by Churchmen generally, that the mass of the Welsh people are estranged from the Establishment. Judge Johns, in his able essay on the causes of Dissent in Wales, says that "before the rise of Methodism in Wales the churches were as little attended by the great mass of the people as now, and that indifference to all religion prevailed as widely then, as Dissent in the present day." In a recent article which appeared in the *Record* newspaper, we find the following statement:—"It is a lamentable fact, which we record with sorrow, that the great bulk of the Welsh people are alienated from the Churh of their fathers." Both the Bishop of Bangor and the Chanceller of the Exchequer, at a meeting lately held at Dwygyfylchi, Carnarvonshire, gave expression to the same sentiment. But it is needless to multiply testimonies to establish a well-known and universally admitted fact. The name by which the Established Church is known in Wales is "The Church of England," and as far as the Welsh people are concerned it is to all intents and purposes the Church of England. Her bishops, most of her dignitaries, and the incumbents of her richest livings, are Englishmen. The service in many Welsh parishes is conducted exclusively in the English language; and in those parishes where both Welsh and English services are held, the most convenient hour of the day is generally given for the English service. The bulk of the congregations is made up of English residents in the Principality and Anglicised Welshmen. The vast majority of the Welsh population look upon the Church as the Church of the English and not theirs. When the Established Church in Wales, after an experiment of three hundred years, finds herself not the Church of the nation, but the Church of a very small minority of it, it is high time for her friends to consider whether her union with the State is an ordinance of God or a device of man. We, as Dissenters, labour for the separation of the Church from the State, not from the remotest wish to destroy and scatter the Episcopal community—God forbid that we should ever desire such a thing!—but from a conviction forced upon us by the history of our own, as well as other State Churches, that the connection of any form of religion with the State, is contrary to the genius of Christianity, incompatible with unrestricted liberty of conscience,—which is the birthright of every man—and tends to obstruct rather than to hasten the conversion of the world.

WELSH DISSENT.

A LETTER TO THE LORD BISHOP OF LLANDAFF, WITH HIS
LORDSHIP'S REPLY.

(Reprinted from the Star of Gwent, Sept. 5, and Sept. 26, 1857.)

To the RIGHT REV. THE LORD BISHOP OF LLANDAFF.

MY LORD BISHOP,—As public men are in some respects public property, it is natural to expect that a vigilant public would watch their movements and criticise their words and actions, and if fairly criticised, in a Christian and gentlemanly spirit, they have no reason to complain.

Considering this, I am persuaded that I shall not violate any rule of propriety by offering a few remarks on some sentences uttered by your Lordship on the 18th instant, at the consecration of the district church at Penmain, Monmouthshire. You are reported in the *Star of Gwent* as having said "that you believed the system of Dissent was nearly worn out in the Welsh districts; that you feared that Welsh Dissent *had now become too much of a political organization;* and that you had little doubt, if the clergy acted up to the spirit of their commission, that the *delusion of Dissent* would soon disappear from amongst them."

It appears to me very strange that a gentleman of your Lordship's reputed keenness of observation and general information, should be so credulous as to believe that Dissent is nearly worn out in the Welsh districts. Permit me to call your Lordship's attention to a few facts which will at once show the groundlessness of your belief. Let us take four of the most populous parishes in the Welsh districts of your diocese as instances.

The parish of Aberystruth has *four* churches and *seventeen* Dissenting chapels, and the attendants at *one* of the chapels greatly outnumber the attendants at the *four* churches. Is Dissent nearly worn out here?

The parish of Bedwellty has *five* churches and *forty-two*

Dissenting chapels. Supposing the five church congregations to be as large as any five of the forty-two Dissenting congregations, which is all that can be supposed, will it follow that the statistics of this parish furnish a proof that Dissent is nearly worn out? .

In the parish of Merthyr Tydvil there are *six* churches and forty-four Dissenting chapels. Supposing again that the six church congregations are as large as any six of the Dissenting congregations, which I hardly think can be the fact, there are no grounds here also for your Lordship to believe that Dissent is nearly worn out.

In the parish of Aberdare there are six churches and thirty-four Dissenting chapels, and the proportion of Churchmen to Dissenters is about the same here as in the other three parishes. It is worthy of notice that of the 137 Dissenting chapels in these four parishes, 75 were built within the last twenty years, and that 25 of the others were rebuilt and greatly enlarged within the same period. The statistics of the other large parishes of the Welsh districts of the diocese, such as Trevethin, Mynyddislwyn, Risca, Eglwysilan, Pentyrch, Llanwono, Llantrisant, Llangynwyd, Aberavon, St. Michael's, Neath, &c., will not furnish your Lordship with any better grounds for your belief. Dissent nearly worn out! Not so, my Lord; it is in the bloom and vigour of its youth, and ten times stronger than it was twenty years ago.

If, by being nearly worn out, your Lordship means that Dissent is in a state of *spiritual declension*, I beg leave to offer a few remarks, but with caution, as the subject is a most delicate one. Your Lordship, I presume, will agree with me that the spirituality of individuals or communities is to be tested, not by certain bodily gestures at public worship, the minute observance of human ceremonies, and the unscrupulous use of any and every means to promote the interest of sects, but by holiness of conduct, heavenly mindedness, amiableness of temper, self-denial, and devotedness to the service of God. It must be confessed, with sorrow, that the spiritual state of the Dissenting churches generally, is far from being what it should be, and what every pious man wishes it to be. Yet no one acquainted with our history will venture to assert that our spiritual state is not at the present time as encouraging as at any former period since the origin of Dissent, with the exception of those happy seasons of revivals, with which we have been repeatedly blessed in this and former ages. The spirituality of the Dissenting ministers and their congregations,. if tested by the forementioned standard, can bear to be compared with advantage with the spirituality of the Established clergy and their congregations; and, therefore, to say that Dissent, in this sense, is nearly worn out, is equivalent to asserting that Christianity itself is nearly worn out.

Your Lordship fears that Welsh Dissent *is now become too much of a political organization.* This fear, my lord, I am happy to tell you, is as groundless as your belief that Dissent is nearly worn out in the Welsh Districts. There are at least four thousand sermons delivered every Lord's day in the Dissenting pulpits of the Principality, and nearly as many on week days, and I can safely challenge any man to prove that the least reference to political matters is introduced into one in a thousand of these sermons from one end of the year to the other. Hundreds of the Dissenting ministers of Wales are surrounded every Sabbath by congregations of eight or ten hundred immortal souls, a large proportion of whom are, we fear, in an unconverted state, and with all our deficiencies, we are not yet so indifferent to the eternal welfare of our fellow-men, as to feel inclined to divert their attention from their dangerous state as lost sinners, by introducing political questions into our sermons, or any of our religious meetings. We feel, and oh! that we felt it more intensely, that our mission is to warn sinners to flee from the wrath to come, and to endeavour to make people zealous, enlightened, and scriptural Christians, not hot-headed politicians. My lord, I assert it boldly, and without fear of contradiction, that the Dissenting ministers of Wales, as a body, and their congregations, are not behind any on the bench of bishops, or among the Established clergy and their congregations, in loyalty and sincere devotedness to the person of our most excellent and dearly beloved Sovereign, and in cheerful obedience to the laws of our country.

Your lordship cannot be ignorant of the fact that to accuse religious people of political designs has ever been, and still is, a common artifice of persecutors, in order to justify their own cruel deeds, and to blacken the character and destroy the influence of their victims. Was not the Saviour of the world himself put to death under the false charge of being a political disturber? Were not the apostles and the primitive Christians most cruelly butchered by the heathen, under the pretence that they formed political organizations to subvert governments? Were not the Waldenses and the Albigenses, from time immemorial, treated with all manner of cruelty as falsely accused political offenders? Were not the dark prisons of England in the seventeenth century crowded by thousands of Puritans and Nonconformists, "men of whom the world was not worthy," under the groundless and libellous charge of forming political organizations? Are not the Protestants of France, and especially of Italy, at this very day annoyed, persecuted, and imprisoned under the same false accusation? And does the Bishop of Llandaff tread in the footsteps of these ancient and modern slanderers of the people of God?

If a Dissenter had said that the Established Church is too much of a political organization, he might have justified his statement with the very conclusive reason that twenty-six of her chief ministers are *ex-officio* members of the legislature, and that nearly half the time of our representatives in the House of Commons is taken up in discussing and ordering her affairs.

"The delusion of Dissent;" and what does your Lordship mean by this? Do you mean the doctrines which we believe and preach? We believe and preach the sufficiency of the Holy Scriptures as a rule of faith and practice in all matters pertaining to religion, to the exclusion of all human injunctions and ceremonies. Is this the delusion of Dissent? We believe and preach the total depravation and ruin of mankind by the fall of the first Adam, and the incarnation, the atoning death, and intercession of the second Adam, as the only means of their recovery. Is this the delusion of Dissent? We believe and preach the necessity of Divine influence to convert sinners, and that man is justified by faith without the works of the law. Is this the delusion of Dissent? We believe and preach that true religion is neither pharisaical sanctimoniousness nor antinomian licentiousness, but a pious principle evincing itself in a holy life. Is this the delusion of Dissent? We do not believe nor preach baptismal regeneration. We neither believe nor preach apostolical succession by virtue of Episcopal ordination. Is this the delusion of Dissent? We consider all those who believe and practice the doctrines and precepts of the Apostles, and who devote themselves with apostolic zeal to disseminate the truth, and to convert sinners from the error of their way, the true successors of the Apostles, whether Episcopally ordained or not. Is this the delusion of Dissent? We attach no importance whatever to the ceremonies of consecrating buildings for the living to worship God, and spots of ground for the dead to be buried. When that celebrated evangelist, Jones of Llangan, was summoned to appear before one of your Lordship's predecessors—Dr. Watson, to answer to the charge brought against him by two clergymen, of preaching in unconsecrated places, his defence was that he believed that the incarnate son of God, the moment he set his foot on our earth, had consecrated every inch of it for preaching his gospel. This is the very belief of all the Dissenters of Wales in the present day. Is this the delusion of Dissent? If by "the delusion of Dissent" your Lordship means all or any of these things, we glory in our delusion, and mean to live and die in it.

A very great change has taken place in the character of the Welsh clergy within the last thirty years. Your Lordship and others may possibly be looking upon it as a change for the better, but a large number of good people within as well as without the pale of the Establishment, consider it a change decidedly for the worse. Amongst the clergy of former ages there were a number of pious men, thoroughly devoted to the duties of their sacred office, while the others, who were merely men of the world, were generally kind-hearted, philanthropic, and good neighbours. The clergy of the present day, with several honourable exceptions, are exclusive, bigoted, and most bitterly sectarian in their spirit, treating their dissenting brethren, not as fellow-labourers in the service of the same great Master, but as enemies and antagonists. My lord, the "deluded" Dissenters of Wales have always been accustomed to consider sectarian exclusiveness and the religion of the New Testament, as two very different and diametrically opposed things, and to look upon the prevalence of the one as anything but an indication of the success of the other. With these views, they cannot but feel truly sorry that a gentleman of your Lordship's age, exalted position, eminent learning, and vast influence, should have said or done anything to foster such a bad and unchristian spirit in your clergy.

If the lay members of the church were half as bigoted and exclusive as some of the clergy are, we could not have sites for our places of worship, nor a foot of ground to bury our dead, and most probably the cruel treatment of Dissenters in the days of Queen Elizabeth and Charles II. would again be repeated in our days. But, through mercy, the gentry of these parts, though members of the Church, are gentlemen of expanded views, perfectly free from sectarian exclusiveness, and always willing to aid and encourage the efforts of Dissenters as well as Churchmen, to promote the interests of religion, education, and morality.

Sir Thomas Phillips, on the occasion on which your Lordship gave utterance to the objectionable sentiments I am commenting upon, instead of misrepresenting and insulting the Dissenters, expressed his wish, in giving the toast, "the Church and the Queen," that the word "church" should be understood in such a wide sense as would evidently include Dissenters as well as Churchmen. This liberality was in every way worthy of that gifted, philanthropic, and liberal gentleman. It would be well for the clergy to receive some lessons on Christian charity from the lay members of their church.

If your Lordship thinks that Dissenters look upon the efforts of Churchmen to do good with a jealous and an envious eye, you will excuse me when I say that you are sadly mistaken. While we deeply regret to witness the growth of sectarian exclusiveness in the Church, we cannot envy it. If "deluded," we are not quite so devoid of love to the Saviour and the souls of men, as not to be able to pray for and rejoice in the success of all pious efforts to save sinners, within the Establishment as well as amongst ourselves. If many of us desire to see the Church separated from the State, we do not desire it from any wish for the destruction of the Episcopal Church, nor the least expectation that that would be the result of the separation; but simply because we consider the connection as unjust and impolitic in its principle, as tending to impede rather than to accelerate the progress of pure religion, and as the means of perpetuating an invidious distinction between one section of the Church of Christ and the other.

If the tree is known by its fruits, Dissent is not such a bad thing as to justify your Lordship's wish for its speedy annihilation. What has it done in your diocese? It has erected above six hundred houses of prayer; it has established about nine hundred or a thousand Sabbath schools to teach the children of the poor gratuitously to read the Word of God; it has attracted multitudes from taverns, dances, and sinful amusements: not from the parish churches, for they were not to be found there. It has been the means of making tens of thousands of the colliers, miners, mechanics, and labourers of the mining and agricultural districts of the counties of Monmouth and Glamorgan not only decent and moral, but eminently pious and well-informed in the highest of all the

K

sciences. If Dissent be of God, and its fruits naturally lead us to infer that it is, all efforts to destroy it will merely be labour thrown away. If your Lordship desires the speedy extinction of Dissent from a wish to see the Church of Christ more united, the piety of your desire cannot be too highly commended, but its wisdom may be doubted. You well know, my lord, that unity and uniformity are not convertible terms. There may be the most rigid uniformity where there is nothing like Christian unity, and there may be the most sincere, evangelical, and heavenly unity, where there is not uniformity. Does not the history of pious people in every age and country prove this?

My lord, is it not evident that Churchmen and Dissenters could be better employed than in slandering, misrepresenting, and quarrelling with one another? Are there not tens of thousands still, after the labours of all parties, of our fellow-men in our large towns and among the teeming population of the mining districts, living and dying in heathen ignorance and sin, at the very thresholds of our churches and chapels? Will it not be soon enough for your Lordship to urge your clergy to make an onslaught on "the delusion of Dissent," after they shall have gathered into the fold of Christ the myriads of drunkards, Sabbath breakers, and careless sinners throughout the diocese, who never enter a place of worship? Why should we not agree to discuss the points on which we differ in a friendly and Christian spirit, and unite our efforts in holy attempts to overthrow the strongholds of sin and Satan?

If I have in the foregoing remarks unfairly commented upon your Lordship's expressions, or made use of any disrespectful words, I can assure you that I did it unintentionally, because I am directed in the Book of my religion to "render honour to whom honour is due," and the instincts of my nature prompt me to be careful not to say or do anything calculated to wound the feelings of any one unnecessarily.

I never expect, my lord, to meet you in this world, but I hope, notwithstanding our present differences, to meet you in heaven, where all the true followers of the Saviour are united in perfect love, and where all their denominational prejudices on earth are eternally forgotten.

I am, my Lord Bishop, yours, most respectfully,
THOMAS REES,

Beaufort, Monmouthshire,   Independent Minister.
August 31, 1857.

Sir,—You will oblige me, and possibly serve the cause of truth and Christian charity, by inserting in the forthcoming number of your paper the following letters, with which I have been favoured by his Lordship the Bishop of Llandaff:—

"At Reading, September 14, 1857.

"Sir,—Your letter to myself, reprinted from the Star of Gwent, has been received by me at this place. Though the circumstance which has brought me hither may perhaps justify me in postponing my acknowledgment of it, I feel unwilling to do so, not merely on account of the subject to which it refers, but also because I am anxious at once, so far as I can, to put myself right, and to thank you for the kind and Christian spirit in which you have been pleased to address me.

"My speech at Penmain was entirely unpremeditated. I had no idea that I should be called upon. Whatever I said, therefore, was strictly speaking, the utterance of the moment. This, of course, would be no excuse for my saying, if I did say, anything untrue, but might possibly account for some expressions not having been weighed as under other circumstances they might have been. I have seen no report of my speech. Any report, if a faithful one, must, I am sure, have contained qualifying sentences, which would go a great way towards removing the impression that I entertained false views of Welsh Dissent, or that I wished to misrepresent it. That I consider the divisions in the body of Christ which exist among us, a very great evil and a powerful instrument, amongst others, in preventing the growth of spiritual religion, I have never denied, and so long as I read my Bible I believe that I never shall. But I have never been backward in acknowledging that Welsh Dissent originated in a religious spirit, at a time when the Church was not doing its duty, and that if it had not been for its instrumentality, under the peculiar circumstances of our district, with our immensely increased population and the insufficient endowments of the Church, many persons must have practically remained in a condition of heathenism. This might be admitted, with a full conviction at the same time that there might have been 'a better way.' In the speech upon which you comment I remember distinctly that I expressed a wish that I might not be misunderstood, and said that I fully believed that there were hundreds and thousands of pious Christians at this day among the Dissenters of Wales.

"With regard to the particular passage that you quote from the Star of Gwent, I beg to say that I entertain a very strong conviction, amounting almost to a certainty that I never used the words 'the delusion of dissent.' The phrase is one which I am never in the habit of using, and I do not believe that, even under the circumstances above referred to, it would have escaped my lips. If I said, as reported, that I feared that Welsh Dissent *had now become too much of a political organization*—though I do not believe I did say it—my meaning was incorrectly expressed.

"Dissent, as I am of course aware, is a religious and not a political organization. If I expressed my fears that, having been originally organized for the exclusive purpose of promoting religion, it now employed its power very much for political purposes, I must acknowledge that my words only conveyed an opinion which, however unwillingly, I have been led by circumstances to form, and which is certainly very extensively entertained. It is a great satisfaction to me to be informed, by a person so intimately acquainted as yourself with Welsh Dissent, that political matters occupy so little of its attention. That it may continue 'to warn sinners to flee from the wrath to come,' and to endeavour to make people 'zealous, enlightened, and scriptural Christians,' and to inculcate those doctrines which you think I may possibly mean by 'the delusion of Dissent,' is my best wish on its behalf.

"Though I think that religion would prosper more amongst us did we constitute one body, than it can so long as there are 'divisions amongst us,' Dissent will certainly not be spoken of by me in other than respectful terms so long as it confines itself to these matters. Neither do I think that my brethren the clergy will disagree with me.

"As I never see the STAR OF GWENT, I was not aware, until I received your pamphlet, that you had addressed a letter to me in reference to the meeting at Penmain. It was not, therefore, in my power to take an earlier opportunity of disclaiming or explaining the expressions imputed to me.

"I remain, Sir, your obedient servant,

"A. LLANDAFF.

"P.S.—My remarks have been confined to the expressions which you have printed in italics as being, I conclude, in your judgment, the most objectionable. With respect to the first sentence quoted by you as to 'the system of Dissent,' I believe that my observation in whatever words it was conveyed, for that I do not recollect, was not upon the 'system,' but 'the spirit' of Welsh Dissent, by which I meant the religious spirit from which it took its rise, and this remark was qualified by the statement to which I before referred.

"Rev. T. Rees, Independent Minister,
    Beaufort, Monmouthshire."

On the receipt of the foregoing letter I wrote to his Lordship to ask his permission to publish it, enclosing the report of his speech at Penmain, together with the letter of your anonymous correspondent, "A Resident of the Diocese of St. David's." The following is his Lordship's reply :—

"At Reading, September 17, 1857.

"SIR,—I beg to say that I have no objection to my letter to yourself being published. The report of my speech which you have been so good as to send me quite confirms my own impressions. The words 'there were hundreds and thousands of Dissenters at the present time, but he believed,' &c., are sufficient to prove my veracity as to what I informed you in my last letter that I really did say ; but are not sufficient to give the reader of the paper any idea of the qualification with which I accompanied my observations as to the present condition of Welsh Dissent. They are enough to prove how unsafe it is to rely upon a newspaper report of words. Whatever be my opinions upon the commission of the clergy— a subject upon which I have no need now to enter—I am perfectly certain that I never said 'who themselves had received the seal of the divine commission,' though I have no doubt that I used the words 'if they acted up to the spirit of their commission.'

"The anonymous letter which you have been so good as to send me will, so far as I am concerned, remain unanswered.

"I am, Sir, your obedient servant,

"A. LLANDAFF.

"P.S.—If you think fit to print this, it may accompany the former letter.

"Rev. T. Rees, Independent Minister,
    Beaufort, Mon."

These explanations will, I am certain, be perfectly satisfactory to all parties, and will remove at once the unpleasant impression which the report of his Lordship's speech has left on the minds of many good people. While as Dissenters we disagree, of course, with his Lordship's views in regard to the Establishment as "a better way" than Dissent, yet we cannot help admiring his most courteous and eminently Christian spirit. May all his clergy and the ministers of all the Dissenting denominations largely imbibe his conciliatory and amicable temper. · A little more mutual understanding between Churchmen and Dissenters would remove the cold, suspicious, and unfriendly feeling which they entertain towards each other, and lead them more to unite their efforts in the promotion of the interests of our common Christianity, which they could easily do without compromising their peculiar principles. His Lordship, and all other respectable Churchmen, I trust will soon feel perfectly convinced that Dissenters, *as religious bodies*, do not and have never been in the habit of meddling with any political questions, *excepting those which immediately affect their religious privileges and liberties*. As individual members of the Commonwealth, no one can object to their using their political rights according to their convictions, like other men.

I am happy to be able to inform his Lordship that the flame of that ardent piety in which Welsh Dissent originated is not yet extinguished amongst us, and if I rightly understand his Lordship's character, he would be one of the last to wish that it should be extinguished, until he could ascertain that it had been re-kindled with equal or greater strength in his own church.

The letters of your anonymous correspondents shall pass unnoticed by me. Christian men should not write a line to which they would be ashamed to append their names.

I am, Sir, yours respectfully,

THOMAS REES,

Beaufort, Sept. 21, 1857.   Independent Minister.

THE CONGREGATIONAL CHURCHES OF WALES.

A PAPER READ AT THE AUTUMNAL MEETING OF THE CONGRE-
GATIONAL UNION OF ENGLAND AND WALES, HELD AT
HALIFAX, OCTOBER, 1858.

CONGREGATIONALISM was the earliest form of Dissent in Wales,
and Congregationalism is still the prevailing form. A Congregational church was formed at Llanvaches, in Monmouthshire, as early as the month of November, 1639, and this was
the first Dissenting church in the Principality. A second was
soon after formed at Mynyddislwyn, in the same county, and
a third at Cardiff, in Glamorganshire.

John Penry, the pilgrim martyr, who sacrificed his life
through his efforts to promote the evangelization of Wales,
never settled as a minister in his native country; and therefore the honour of being the father of Welsh Nonconformity
belongs to the Rev. William Wroth, B.A., minister of the
church at Llanvaches. He was born in Monmouthshire, in
the year 1570, was educated at Jesus College, Oxford, and
was appointed rector of the parish of Llanvaches in the year
1600, or possibly two or three years earlier. He began to
preach the Gospel with great earnestness about the year 1603.
His fame soon spread around, and vast numbers of serious
people, from six or seven of the adjoining counties of England
and Wales, attended his ministry at Llanvaches. In the
summer months he was obliged to preach in the churchyard,
as the church could not contain only a small proportion of the
multitudes who flocked to hear him.

During the primacy of Archbishop Abbot, this zealous
Puritan, amongst many others, was permitted unmolested to
enjoy his benefice as minister of the Established church, but,
directly after the elevation of Laud to the see of Canterbury,
he was proceeded against, in the Court of High Commission,
as "a noted schismatic." His crimes were, preaching the
Gospel with Puritan earnestness, and refusing to read the
"Book of Sports." Immediately after his ejectment from the
Establishment, he formed a Dissenting church, "according to

the model of the Independents;" and this afterwards, as an old historian remarks, "was, like Antioch, the mother-church in that Gentile country, being very famous for her officers, members, order, and gifts."

Mr. Wroth's ministry was blessed to the conversion of many young men, who, during and after his time, became eminent evangelists in Wales, such as William Erbury, Walter Cradock, Richard Symonds, Henry Walter, Ambrose Mostyn, Vavasor Powell, and others. Shortly before the civil wars, Mr. Wroth, according to his desire, was removed to a better world. Soon after, the nonconforming ministers of Wales, and most of the male members of their churches, fled into England, to avoid being pressed into the King's army by the Commission of Array, leaving behind them only elderly men, women, and children. These poor and defenceless people were most cruelly treated by the King's party, but they stood unswervingly to their principles. When Walter Cradock returned to Wales, in the year 1646, he found that the few persecuted people, whom he had left four years before, had been going diligently from house to house, amidst the ravages of the civil wars, and without the aid of any ordained minister, to proclaim the truths of the Gospel to their benighted countrymen; and that they had been the means of converting eight hundred souls around the then thinly-inhabited mountains on the borders of the counties of Monmouth and Brecknock.

Previous to the civil wars all the Nonconformists of Wales were Congregational Pædobaptists, but during the wars some of the Welsh refugees in England were converted to Anti-pædobaptist views, and these, when they returned to their native country, after the subjugation of the Royalists, propagated their new views, and succeeded in setting up a second Dissenting denomination; but it does not appear that they were remarkably numerous, nor that they had any men of eminence amongst them until the year 1655, when they were joined by the celebrated Vavasor Powell. Ever since that time the Anti-pædobaptists in Wales have gradually gained strength, and at the present day they are, next to the Congregationalists, the largest and most flourishing Dissenting body in South Wales.

During the interregnum, the Gospel was preached with remarkable power and glorious effect through the length and breadth of the Principality. Owing to the scarcity of qualified ministers able to preach in the Welsh language, a number of

pious and talented laymen were sent out as itinerant preachers.
About twenty of the members of the Congregational churches
at Llanvaches and Mynyddislwyn were employed in this
service.   Notwithstanding the sneers and contempt with
which prejudiced Church historians treat the names and
labours of Walter Cradock, Vavasor Powell, their fellow-
labourers and assistants, the effects of their work demonstrate
that they did immeasurably more to evangelize Wales, during
this brief period, than all the Episcopal clergy did during the
previous hundred years.   When the reading of the "Book of
Sports" was enforced by Charles I. in 1633, there were only
three clergymen in the whole of Wales who had the courage
and the piety to disobey the King's impious command; those
were William Wroth, William Erbury, and Walter Cradock;
but, when Charles II. enforced the Act of Uniformity in 1662,
we find one hundred and six Welsh ministers ejected from
their livings for refusing to acknowledge the King's authority
over their consciences.   To what are we to attribute this
change in the character of the Welsh clergy, in the short period
of twenty-nine years, if not to the pious labours of the Welsh
evangelists during the time of the Long Parliament and the
Protectorate of Cromwell?

The ministers ejected in Wales by the Act of Uniformity,
were men of ardent piety, courageous spirits, and unwearied
perseverance.   They traversed almost every district of the
Principality during the persecuting reigns of Charles II. and
James II. preaching in forests, caves, barns, farm-houses, and
even in prisons.   Their self-denying labours were not in vain
in the Lord.   Thousands were converted through their ministry,
and when the Act of Toleration came into force, several
chapels were erected, hundreds of dwelling houses recorded for
preaching, and the cause of evangelical religion silently but
steadily progressed.

Dissent in Wales has generally been represented as fast
dying away previous to the rise of Calvinistic Methodism, but
this representation is far from being correct.   It will be
readily conceded that the Dissenting churches in Wales, as
well as in England, at that time were not so active and
energetic as the circumstances of the time required; but to
say that they were feeble, decaying, and dying away, is
untrue.   Calvinistic Methodism in Wales is as much an offshoot
from the existing Dissenting churches as from the Established
church.   The clerical leaders of the movement were members

of the Establishment; but the first "exhorters," or lay preachers, many of whom were equal to the clergy in preaching talents, were almost all trained up under Congregational ministers, and were members of Congregational churches. The Dissenting churches of those times, if they had no Sabbath schools in the modern form, had Bible classes and stated meetings for catechising young people; and they were particularly careful to instruct their youth in the principles of religion. Such was their care, in this respect, that the Methodists represented them as having nothing but intellectual religion, while they, on the other hand, represented the Methodists as ignorant enthusiasts, insisting only upon experimental religion, to the entire neglect of the intellect. Both parties, it seems, ran somewhat to extremes on these points. The clerical Methodists would never have been able to establish the Calvinistic Methodist Connexion in Wales, had it not been for the hundreds of well-instructed members of Dissenting churches who joined them at the outset, to form the nucleus of their first societies. It was not in North Wales, where Dissent was feeble and uninfluential, and where the mass of the population remained in Popish ignorance, that Calvinistic Methodism made its first appearance, but in South Wales, where the Dissenting Churches were comparatively numerous, strong, and efficient. Howell Harries, the first Methodist preacher in Wales, was born, bred, and began his ministry in Breconshire, where, in a population not exceeding 15,000, there were above 3,000 avowed Dissenters, and three large Dissenting churches within two or three miles of the place of his birth. Daniel Rowlands, the first Methodistic clergyman in the Principality, began his ministry in Cardiganshire, in the immediate neighbourhood of five Congregational churches, with nearly 1,000 communicants, and presided over by three learned, pious, and efficient ministers. William Williams, "the Welsh Watts," another clerical Methodist, was brought up in a Congregational church, of which his parents were members, and was educated at the Congregational seminary at Llwynllwyd, in Radnorshire. The Congregational churches of Wales, including a few Presbyterian congregations, and exclusive of the Anti-pædobaptist churches, in the year 1717, were sixty-seven in number, with sixty-four ministers, and 16,000 hearers. Considering that the population of the Principality at that time was less than one-fifth of its present amount, 16,000 was not by any means a con-

temptibly small number. Our churches in 1742 were eighty-
eight in number. I mention these facts, not with the least
desire to rob Calvinistic Methodism of a single gem rightly
belonging to its crown, but to show that the original Dissenting churches did more to evangelize the Principality than
they are generally represented to have done.

The novelty of the Methodist movement, and the encouragement given by its clerical leaders to laymen to excercise their
gifts as preachers—a practice blameably discouraged by the
Congregational ministers of that age—naturally induced a
large number of the most active members of our churches to
join the new denomination. The zeal of all the friends of
evangelical truth for the peculiar doctrines of grace was also
rekindled by the Calvinistic Methodist revival, and had the
effect of driving a few congregations and ministers, who were
nominally Presbyterian, and who had previously embraced
Arminianism, to Arianism, and ultimately to Unitarianism.
These things for a time retarded the progress of our churches,
but in the course of a few years they recovered from the
effects of these reverses, and began with renewed strength to
gain ground. The number of the Welsh Congregational
churches in 1773 amounted to 101.

About the close of the eighteenth century a considerable
number of young men entered the ministry. Many of these
exhibited a happy combination of the fire of the Methodist
and the learning of the Dissenter, Among these worthies the
most noted was the late David Davies of Swansea, who was
not as a preacher in any respect inferior to George Whitfield,
in the estimation of competent judges who frequently heard
both. The powerful ministry of this eloquent man and his
celebrated contemporaries, aroused the whole country. New
interests were formed, and new chapels erected in every
direction; and a wide-spread revival, which commenced in
the year 1807, and lasted for two or three years, vastly
increased the membership of the churches.

Our denomination was very feeble and scarcely known in
most parts of North Wales until the beginning of this century;
when through the labours of the learned Dr. George Lewis,
the pious John Roberts of Llanbrynmair, the seraphic Williams
of Wern, the talented David Morgan of Llanfyllin, and some
others, the few old churches planted by the ejected ministers
were revived, and several additional congregations were
gathered; but as the Calvinistic Methodists had the whole of

the northern part of the Principality almost entirely to themselves for above fifty years, they are still more than double our number there.

The number and strength of the churches of our denomination were more than trebled during the general and most powerful revivals which occurred in the years 1828, 1839, and 1849. In the last of these blessed visitations about ten thousand members were added to them, in parts of four counties of South Wales. The present number of the Welsh Congregational churches, including eighteen in England, is 740, and of the ministers and preachers 612. The communicants are about 75,000; and the regular attendants who are not church members, may be estimated at about 130,000.*

The Calvinistic Methodists are justly entitled to the honour of having taken the lead in the establishment of Sabbath schools in the modern form in Wales. They did more in promoting this good work, in the close of the last and the beginning of this century, than all the other denominations united; but ours, and the other religious bodies, soon copied their good example. At present, all our churches have their Sabbath schools, and they are as numerously attended and as efficiently conducted as those of any denomination, excepting the Calvinistic Methodists, who hitherto maintain a pre-eminent position as promoters of Sabbath-school instruction. All the members of our churches, both young and old, are expected to attend the Sabbath school, and few, if any, who are esteemed good and active Christians, neglect to do so. We have no paid teachers, and it would be as repugnant to the feelings of our people to pay persons for teaching classes in the Sabbath school, as it would be to pay them for attending the prayer-meeting or the Lord's Supper. There may be cases where paid teachers are essential to the very existence of Sabbath schools, but such cases are not known in Wales, at least within the circles of the Dissenting communities..

There are some things which I presume are peculiar to our

---

* Our churches have greatly increased in number and strength since the above statement was written. Their statistics at the close of the year 1866 were as follows:—chapels, 877; churches, 808; members, 90,534; hearers, 118,546; total of members and hearers, 209,080; Sunday School scholars, 95,470; teachers, 11,960; annual contributions, £59,616; ordained ministers, 449; students and lay preachers, 396; county and borough voters, 9,319.

churches in the Principality, a notice of which may not be
uninteresting ⬤ our English brethren.   One of these peculiarities is our itinerant preaching.   Any recognised minister of
our denomination could send at any time to the ministers or
the deacons of all our churches, from Cardiff to Holyhead, to
ask them to announce him to preach in their pulpits on
the days and the hours he might name, and no one would
consider him an intruder by so doing.   Of course, as Independents, we have no law to bind the churches in this matter ;
but this is the custom, and the universal understanding
amongst us.   All our popular ministers throughout the Principality spend, on an average, a month or six weeks every
year in visiting the churches as itinerant preachers.   We
generally go out, like the seventy disciples, "two and two,"
preaching, especially in rural districts, two or three times
every day.   Every church has its separate fund, for what we
call the occasional ministry, out of which the travelling
expenses of the itinerants are paid.   Our churches are so far
from feeling this custom to be burdensome, that they would
consider its entire discontinuance a great calamity.   The
opinion is generally entertained amongst us that this itinerant
preaching is highly beneficial in different ways—that it
improves the preaching talents of the ministers themselves,
that it revives and cheers the churches which they visit, and
that it keeps both ministers and churches from that cold
isolation and estrangedness, which are anything but consistent
with the loving and sociable spirit of Christianity.   This,
like every other good custom, is not without its abuses.   Some
persons, whose preaching talents, and conversation in the
families where they are entertained, are by no means edifying,
avail themselves of this liberty to visit the churches, to whom,
of course, they are not welcome visitors ; but these characters
are not numerous, and our people, rather than forego the
privilege of hearing popular ministers, quietly tolerate this
inconvenience.

The Society meeting is another peculiarity.   Every church
has a meeting of this kind held once or twice weekly.   None
but the members of the church and the candidates for membership attend it.   These meetings are similar to the Wesleyan
classes, with this difference, that the minister always presides,
and that all the members, and not a select number, are
expected to attend them.   The pastor, after delivering a short
opening address, invites the deacons and other elderly persons,

to state their religious experience, or to give appropriate exhortations to different classes, such as heads of families, the aged, the young, masters, servants, the poor or the afflicted. Occasionally, the members are addressed personally, in the presence of the whole Society, and encouraged, warned, or directed, according to their different characters. These meetings are considered by' all evangelical Dissenting denominations in Wales as the most important and useful of our religious services. Those churches who practically neglect them are the least spiritual and efficient, and those members of our churches who seldom or never frequent them, are generally the most inactive and worthless professors we have. Such is the high estimation in which we hold the Society meeting, that we would look upon its discontinuance in any church as a certain sign of the decay, and a prelude of the ultimate ruin of that church.

We have also our quarterly and annual Associations. A meeting is held every three months, in each county, which continues for two days. The ministers and the delegates of the churches hold a conference for two or three hours on the morning of the first day, when all subjects connected with the general welfare of the denomination in the county are discussed. The remainder of the first day, and the whole of the second, are devoted to preaching. Two, and sometimes three short sermons are delivered at each service. The chapels are always crowded on such occasions. We have also our annual Associations, nine of which are held every year in the different counties of South and North Wales. These, like the quarterly meetings, are continued for two days. At a conference, on the first morning, all the ministers present are expected to give some account of the spiritual state of their churches, and of their increase or decrease during the past year. Two services for preaching are held the first day, and four on the second. At each service two or three sermons are delivered. All the services, when the weather permits, are held in the open air. The preachers stand on a platform, erected on a field for the occasion. These meetings, especially in the western counties of South Wales, are attended by immense numbers of people. We have often witnessed ten, twelve, and even fifteen thousand assembled on such occasions, and we have not unfrequently found that to speak so as to make all in such vast crowds to hear, was not a slight exercise for the lungs. Our general opinion is, that these meetings,

like our itinerant preaching, are calculated to do much good
to both ministers and people.

That these peculiarities of ours have done wonders in
the promotion of evangelical religion in Wales is unquestionable; but I am not competent to decide whether similar
methods would suit other countries, where the state of society
and the habits of the people are different. Whatever may be
the opinions entertained of our plans of furnishing our countrymen with the means of religious knowledge, we have the
satisfaction to find that our humble efforts, through the Divine
blessing, have succeeded in bringing the great mass of the
middle and labouring classes throughout the whole Principality under the influence of the Gospel. The number of
those who never attend the means of grace, scarcely amounts
to ten per cent. of the Welsh population.

We have, amongst the Congregational ministers of Wales,
some of the most striking instances of ministerial activity and
success. I shall specify two or three. When the Rev. David
Rees was ordained at Llanelly, Carmarthenshire, in the year
1828, the only Congregational chapel in the town was small
and inelegant; and the church, consisting only of the labouring class, had not above 140 members. Mr. Rees has since
twice enlarged his chapel, and at present it is one of the most
elegant Dissenting chapels in the Principality, containing
1,000 sittings. This indefatigable minister has also built four
additional chapels in and within two miles of the town. Our
denomination has now, at Llanelly, five chapels, with 3,500
sittings. The communicants exceed 1,200. The spacious
chapels are crowded by attentive hearers, and four ministers
are comfortably supported, where, in 1828, scarcely one could
be supported. All this has been accomplished within thirty
years, in a town whose population does not exceed 12,000.

The Rev. William Ambrose was ordained at Portmadoc,
Carnarvonshire, twenty-two years ago. Both the chapel and
congregation were very small at that time. The congregation
soon increased, and the chapel was rebuilt and greatly enlarged.
That neat edifice has again become too small, and is forthwith
to be re-enlarged. Mr. Ambrose has also erected four additional chapels in different districts of the neighbourhood,
which are well attended.

The Rev. John Davies settled at Aberaman, Glamorganshire,
four years ago. During the first year of his pastorate, the
chapel was enlarged to nearly double its former size; in the

second year he built a new chapel, in an adjoining populous district, where there is now an increasing self-supporting church, and this year he has formed a third church in another part of the neighbourhood. These are only a few out of many similar instances which might be specified. · Wales is more indebted, under God, to the activity and disinterestedness of ministers, for the general spread of religion through the land, than to all other things combined; but the fact should not be concealed, that our denomination has also lost ground in many important districts, through the selfishness and inactivity of ministers.

The ministers of our denomination have contributed their full share to the literature of Wales. They have furnished unabridged translations of Henry on the Bible, and of Guyse, Burkitt, and Barnes on the New Testament; two original Commentaries, of considerable value, on the New Testament; two Biblical Dictionaries, two Theological Dictionaries, a valuable Ecclesiastical History, the only one in the language, with small volumes, single sermons, and pamphlets on different theological and general subjects without number. We have five denominational Periodicals, with a monthly circulation of 16,000. Some thousands of the "Evangelical Magazine," the "Christian Witness," and other English Periodicals, are also circulated monthly amongst our people. Two of our ministers are editors of weekly Welsh newspapers. The Welsh nation, from time immemorial, have been very proud of their poets. We have, at the present time, six or seven poets of national fame, and four of these are Congregational ministers. One of our ministers is the author of the only oratorio ever published in Wales, and several of the members of our churches are known throughout the nation as masters in the science of sacred music. I am happy to be able to state that we have no such thing as Infidel literature in our language.

Ministerial education has received the particular attention of our churches from a very early period in the history of our denomination. The first seminary in Wales was established at Brynllwarch, in Glamorganshire, under the learned Samuel Jones, A.M., soon after the memorable year 1662. Two or three similar institutions were opened in other parts of the Principality by learned Congregational ministers, before the close of the seventeenth century. The college at Carmarthen was established in the beginning of the eighteenth century, and was jointly supported for fifty years by the London

Congregational and Presbyterian Boards. That venerable institution, for some generations, has been under the exclusive control of the Unitarians, but they have liberally allowed the theological chair to be filled for the last seventy years by Congregational ministers, and the majority of the students from time to time have been Congregationalists. The Independent College at Brecon, which was established at Abergavenny in the year 1753, is most efficiently conducted.* A very useful preparatory institution was also opened at Bala, in North Wales, some years ago. Ours, including a small number of Presbyterian churches, which could scarcely be considered a distinct body, was the only Dissenting denomination in Wales which had any thing to do with ministerial education in the seventeenth and eighteenth centuries. In the present century, the Anti-pædobaptists and the Calvinistic Methodists have followed our example. We have been blessed with a succession of tutors equally eminent for learning and piety; such as Samuel Jones, A.M., Rees, Prytherch, William Evans, James Owen, Vavasor Griffiths, Evan Davies, Thomas Perrot, David Peter, and Drs. Benjamin Davies, Edward Williams, George Lewis, Jenkin Lewis, &c.

Our people are rapidly improving in their liberality. The incomes of ministers have been greatly advanced of late years, and though still unreasonably low, not averaging above £60 a-year, yet if the churches will improve in their liberality in the ensuing twenty years, at the same rate as they have done in the last twenty, we shall not have much cause to complain. Our people have contributed, during the last twenty years, at least £15,000 annually towards the erection of chapels. Our missionary contributions last year amounted to £2,300, and our collections towards the colleges to above £1,200. These sums may appear small when compared with the number of the churches, but it should be understood that we have no princely merchants, nor a single extensive landed proprietor, amongst us; that our congregations are made up exclusively of the middle and working classes; and that we support above 700 distinct interests, in a population nearly 200,000 less than

---

* The Congregational Fund Board, London, after withdrawing its assistance from the college at Carmarthen, in 1753, annually voted liberal sums to support the Independent College, which is now at Brecon; and that Institution derives still above a third part of its entire income from this source. No Welshman should be ignorant of this fact.

that of the West Riding of Yorkshire, or the Southern division of Lancashire.

The spiritual state of the churches is at the present time, upon the whole, highly encouraging. We have no powerful revivals, but all our Societies are peaceful, and most of them on the increase. The Gospel is preached in its purity everywhere amongst us. There is not, to my knowledge, one individual amongst our 612 recognised ministers and preachers whose orthodoxy is suspected. This does not arise from our entire ignorance of unsound German, English, and American literature. Many of us have read the productions of most of the leading infidel and rationalistic writers of the age, but we have not yet met with a sufficient reason for renouncing those blessed Gospel doctrines, by the preaching of which the Welsh were raised from the depths of Popish superstition to be one of the most enlightened Protestant nations in Christendom.

Whatever may be our excellencies, we are not without our blemishes and deficiences, and honesty demands that they should be noticed. One of our most glaring defects is our apathy and want of energetic co-operation in the establisment of efficient day schools. We have many good British and Denominational schools in the Principality, but not one-tenth of what is necessary. We are disagreed amongst ourselves on the subject of Government education; and while we are discussing the matter, without establishing a sufficient number of voluntary schools, nor accepting Government aid, the Established Church comes forward, devouring the Grants of Government, by the tens of thousands, for establishing Church schools in the midst of Dissenting populations.

We have also been very backward in using our political rights properly. Our ministers are often branded by bigoted Churchmen as political firebrands, and our churches as political clubs; but the simple fact that all our representatives are Churchmen, most of them Conservatives of the old school, while three-fourths of the electors are Dissenters, is a sufficient refutation of this base slander. The truth is, we have culpably neglected to assert our political rights, leaving our brethren in England to fight the battles of religious liberty unaided by us.

In some cases we have multiplied chapels unnecessarily. When churches happened to quarrel with their ministers or amongst themselves, additional chapels were erected in thinly populated districts, by which our cause has been weakened

M

and disgraced. There may be twenty or thirty cases of this description in South and North Wales, but nothing of the kind has occurred lately; and may it never occur again.

I have one point more to advert to, and a point of the greatest interest. In many districts of the Principality the state of society is just now passing through an important change, by the rapid increase of the English population, and the consequent prevalence of the English language. Nothing will prevent the utter extinction of our interests in those districts but the immediate establishment of efficient English preaching. We have been taught by experience that English and Welsh services in the same chapels will never answer. The necessary brevity of this paper will not permit me to enter into details respecting the places where English preaching is most wanted, and the best ways of supplying them. I shall merely take the liberty of suggesting that the most efficient plan which occurs to me would be the appointment of a Special Committee, to be composed of an equal number of English and Welsh brethren, acting under the sanction of the Congregational Union, to take the case of the English population of Wales under consideration. We have no need of a new society for this purpose, as the Home Missionary and the English Congregational Chapel-Building Societies are well adapted to meet the case, if their operations were directed by a Special Committee. I repeat it most emphatically, that something must be done, and done immediately, in this matter, otherwise the interest of our denomination in Wales, and even the cause of evangelical religion, will inevitably suffer.

The Welsh churches have been considered, from the formation of the Congregational Union, as an integral part of it; but their affairs have not hitherto had that prominence in its proceedings which their importance deserves. We Welshmen have none to blame for this but ourselves. We have always found our English brethren kind, sociable, and ready to embrace us, whenever we expressed a desire to associate with them; but we have kept ourselves too much aloof from their society. May our mutual intercourse and intimacy in future be closer than ever. Beloved English brethren, we may learn many important lessons by associating with you, and you may learn something of us. With all our defects, we have no ground to suspect that you are ashamed to own us. Backward as we have been in aiding your laudable efforts to promote the cause of perfect religious liberty, we have furnished you with a triumphant argument to confute those who assert, in and out of Parliament, that the expenses of religious worship cannot be met in rural districts without compulsory rates. You can safely direct those gentlemen to ·Wales, where they will find the poorest and most rural districts in the kingdom, and challenge them to point out a single nook, corner, dingle, hill, or vale, from Cardiff to Holyhead, and from St. David's to Radnor, where there is not a place of worship suitable to the locality, built and kept in repair without any compulsory rate. If we are not able to support your noble institutions for the evangelization of the nations, with our tens of thousands annually, we are willing to cast our mites into the treasury; and tens of thousands of our sincere and earnest prayers meet yours daily at the throne of heaven, for the advancement and final triumph of the Redeemer's kingdom throughout the world.

THE CONGREGATIONAL CHURCHES AND THE ENGLISH POPULATION OF WALES.

A PAPER READ BEFORE THE CONGREGATIONAL UNION AT BRISTOL, OCTOBER THE 24TH, 1865.

NONCONFORMITY in Wales, and in the city of Bristol, rose about the same time, and partly through the instrumentality of the same ministers. The apostolic William Wroth, of Llanvaches, near Chepstow, the first Nonconformist minister in Wales, and his younger fellow-labourers, if not the actual founders of Nonconformity in Bristol, were, to say the least, its principal nursing fathers in its very infancy. The writer of "The Broadmead Records," referring to the period from the year 1600 to 1640 says, "There were raised up divers holy and powerful ministers and preachers, in and about that time, in this nation; whereof in these parts was one Mr. Wroth, in Monmouthshire, not far from this city of Bristol, who for the powerfulness and efficaciousness of his preaching, with the exemplary holiness of his life, was called the Apostle of Wales; for the Papists, and all sorts almost, honoured him

for a holy man. By his ministry it pleased the Lord to convert many, so that they left their sinful courses in the world;
after which he caused them to separate from the worship of
the world, and gathered them into the Gospel order of Church-
government, which light of theirs began to shine very much
in this part of the land." Again, referring to the death of
Mr. Yeamans, a Puritan Minister of Bristol, the same writer
says, "The good people were at a great loss, and, like sheep
without a shepherd, were scattered, and knew not where to
hear. But sometimes Mr. Wroth, before mentioned, would
come over, who lodged, when in Bristol, at the house of
William Listun; and sometimes others of the reforming ministers of South Wales, as Mr. Symonds, Mr. Cradock, Mr.
Henry Walter, Mr. Mostyn, and others, would come. But
when they came to town, the professors would run after them,
as hungry souls for food; and sometimes some of the professors of Bristol would go over to Wales, to hear Mr. Wroth
and the good ministers there, so lively were they in those
times, so that the Lord by one and by another built, and
increased them still. Reformation in separation went on."

The month of November in the year 1639, is memorable in
the annals of Welsh Nonconformity, as the time when Mr.
Wroth, then ejected from his living as Vicar of Llanvaches,
formed a large number of persons, converted under his
ministry, into a Congregational church, which was the first
Nonconforming church in the Principality. From that time
to the present, Nonconformity in Wales has had to pass
through many a fiery ordeal and various changes, some of
which were favourable and some otherwise. Yet, in spite of
all adverse circumstances, the oppositions of its enemies, and
some glaring mistakes of its friends, it has from age to age so
steadily gained ground as to become long since emphatically
the national form of religion.

In reviewing the history of the Congregational body in the
Principality from the formation of Mr. Wroth's church in
1639 to the present time, we are inevitably led to the conclusion, that want of zeal, a keen discernment of the signs of
the times, and readiness to adopt measures suited to the ever-
changing state of things, on the part of its leading ministers
and laymen, have proved beyond comparison more disastrous
to its interests, from time to time, than the most violent
opposition of its bitterest enemies. Soon after the Nonconformists obtained liberty of worship under the Act of Toler-

ation, our forefathers directed their attention almost exclusively to ministerial education, neglecting the still more urgent work of evangelizing the ignorant and perishing masses around them. Zeal for a learned ministry became quite a mania with them at that time. We find in some old chapel trust-deeds a provision that none but regularly trained men would be eligible for the pastorate. Piety, activity, eloquence, and respectable natural talent, were regarded as almost worthless, in the absence of a regular training at a theological academy. This extravagant zeal for what was good and desirable in its proper place produced the most disastrous effects. It made the churches proud, apathetic, and non-aggressive, and the ministers cold, formal, and more anxious to maintain their professional respectability than to save souls. In many cases the minister, in order to please one or two genteel families who might be members of his congregation, would conduct the service in the English language, while the bulk of the people understood only the Welsh language. Such was the general state of things in the Congregational churches of Wales from the year 1690 to 1735; and, had it not been for the self-denying labours of a few zealous ministers, who were regarded by their formal brethren as irregular enthusiasts, and the timely outbreak of the great Methodist revival, our body in the Principality, after nobly surviving the persecuting reigns of the Stuarts, would have been ridden to death by a cold formality and a lifeless learned ministry. At the later periods of the eighteenth century, when new measures were introduced for the advancement of religion, such as lay and itinerant preaching, Sabbath-schools, societies, or experience meetings, annual associations, quarterly and monthly meetings of ministers, &c., many of the leading men in the Congregational body either opposed them, or adopted them with such reluctance and slowness, as gave to other denominations opportunities to occupy the ground which they might and ought to have possessed, as the oldest and strongest Dissenting body in the country. Let these mistakes of our forefathers be a warning to us, their descendants. We have not had much cause to complain of denominational apathy and inactivity since the beginning of the present century. The Congregationalists of Wales have worked well during the last sixty years. They have not allowed themselves to be behind any other religious body for zeal, activity, and promptitude to adapt their modes of action to the requirements of the times.

Dissent has now become so prevalent in Wales that no denomination has much more new ground to gain, as far as the Welsh population is concerned, unless we should condescend as religious parties to imitate the Pharisees of old, by going to compass sea and land to make proselytes from one another; for every town, village, and hamlet has places of worship connected with one or other of the leading denominations. No Welsh-speaking inhabitant of the Principality can excuse his ignorance of religion under the plea that the means of grace are not within his reach.

Yet, far be it from us to dream that our work is done when we have thus filled the whole land with Welsh chapels, Welsh ministers, and Sabbath-schools, and that we have nothing more to do but to rest and be thankful. We have still an important, difficult, and expensive work to accomplish, and the accomplishment of which will require nearly as much earnestness, perseverance, self-denial, and energy as our forefathers had to exercise in performing the arduous duties of their times. That great work is to provide an efficient English ministry, attractive places of worship, schools and other means of religious instruction throughout all those districts where the English language prevails. Such is the momentous importance of this work that, unless it be carried on with vigour, earnestness, and promptitude, Congregational Dissent in the most populous, wealthy, and cultivated parts of the country will, in less than thirty years, either die out or become so feeble and obscure, as not to be felt and seen as a power for good in the community. The country is in a state of transition. Englishmen, English capital and enterprise, English customs, and, unhappily, English vices, with very little English virtue and religion, are rushing in upon us, like mighty irresistible torrents, carrying away before them our ancient language, social habits, and even our religious customs and influence over the masses. Our seaport and manufacturing towns have more than doubled their populations within the last twenty years. Quiet localities and secluded valleys where, ten years ago, nothing was to be heard from sunrise to sunset, but the bleating of sheep, the barking of the shepherd's dog, the song of a ploughman here and there, or the melodious notes of the girls singing their morning and evening hymns while milking the cows, have now their quiet disturbed day and night by the ceaseless noise of machineries, coal trains, and thousands of mechanics and labourers toiling for their daily bread. The exhaustless mineral and other resources of our mountains and valleys are as yet only beginning to be developed. The increase of our trade, wealth, and population within the next twenty years, will, beyond question, far exceed the expectations of the most sanguine.

Capitalists, railway companies, merchants, and tradesmen understand the signs of the times, are busily making their calculations, and contriving how they may secure to themselves a good share of the immense wealth of the country. Would God that we as a religious body were as wise in our generation as the children of this world! A few of our ministers and laymen have, for years, felt the need of earnest and combined action for the establishment of English congregations in Wales. Mr. Thomas Thompson, now of Bath, met the Welsh ministers of Monmouthshire, at Beaufort, in the year 1853, where a conference on the subject was held, at which Mr. Thompson generously proposed to give £150 a year for two or three years to assist the infant English interests at Brynmawr, Ebbw-vale, and Beaufort. Conferences were afterwards repeatedly held at Merthyr, Swansea, Cardiff, and Newport; at some of which Mr. Samuel Morley, Mr. Charles Jupe, Mr. John Crossley, Mr. H. O. Wills, and our deeply lamented friend Mr. W. D. Wills, honoured us with their presence, and encouraged us with their most liberal contributions. At a Conference held at Cardiff, about five years ago, a society was formed to co-operate with the Home Missionary and the English Chapel-building Societies, in the support of an English ministry and the erection of Chapels in South Wales and Monmouthshire. That Society, with an annual income of less than £300, has already done wonders, but not one-tenth of what it would have done had it been adequately supported. Fourteen newly-formed or weak churches have been more or less assisted by it within the last four years.

Only a very small number of the Welsh ministers and churches, have as yet entered into this movement with that hearty earnestness which its importance deserves and demands, but the few who have joined it have acted their part well. It requires not a small amount of the grace of self-denial for a minister to persuade a dozen or twenty of the most intelligent, respectable, and wealthy members of his church to separate and form the nucleus of an English cause in the neighbourhood, and afterwards to urge his people to contribute annually to raise the salary of the English minister to £80 or £90 a year, while his own may be ten or twenty pounds under that sum.   Nor are the sacrifices which the people make in following their minister's advice less commendable.   In becoming the founders of a new interest, they more than treble the expense of their worship, while to a Welshman, accustomed from his infancy to hear the Gospel in his own euphonious, strong, and expressive language, to sit under an English ministry is anything but agreeable.   I have not stated an imaginary case, but what has repeatedly taken place in Wales of late years.   The Rev. William Williams, of Hirwaen, and his good people, have furnished us with an instance of such disinterestedness as late as last year.   We are confident that the earnestness of the friends of this movement, together with repeated appeals to the consciences of those Welsh brethren, who have hitherto stood merely as idle spectators, will ere long draw them out to take part with us in the great work of the age.

The interests aided or originated by our Society are all, with two or three exceptions, in villages and the populous vicinities of the iron and coal works, where none but the working classes are to be expected to make up the congregations.   The want of funds has hitherto deterred us from attempting to do anything in the large towns; but unless we can establish ourselves in those centres of wealth and influence, our means and power to do good to the working classes of the villages and manufacturing districts, will soon be at an end.   If Congregationalism in Wales is to have its fair share of the wealth, the intelligence, and the social respectability of the community, we must forthwith secure for ourselves prominent positions in the large towns, which is the case but very partially at present.   Swansea and its suburbs, with nearly 60,000 inhabitants, two-thirds of whom speak the English language, have only one English congregation, while we have nine Welsh congregations for the remaining one-third of the population.   Cardiff, with a population of more than 40,000, has only one respectable English Church, when it ought to have three or four.   £8,000 should at once be laid out in chapel-building in these towns,—a large sum, certainly, but it would be profitably invested; for most probably it would be repaid with interest in fifteen or twenty years, in the assistance which the congregations there would render to establish religious interests elsewhere.

We appeal to you, English friends, for help to carry on our great work. You can help us; you ought to help us, and we are confident that you will help us when our case is fully and fairly laid before you. There are several ways in which you can render us assistance. We need your pecuniary assistance. Besides the sums which we require for chapel-building, our Society, before it will be in efficient working order, must have an annual income of £1,000. It is certain that the Welsh churches will soon be awakened to such a sense of their duty as to raise £500 a year of that sum. Will you meet us with the other £500? If fifty of your wealthiest churches will not subscribe ten pounds each, are there not as many generous ladies and gentlemen throughout England that will respond to our appeal?

You may also very materially help us by using all your influence as ministers and deacons, with such members of your churches as may be lead by their professions or occupations to settle in Wales, to persuade them to be faithful to their principles as Nonconformists. Numbers of educated persons of the middle class come, year after year, from England to occupy positions of respectability and influence in the Principality. We find that many of these gentlemen were members of Congregational churches in England, but on their arrival in Wales, they, almost without exception, renounce their Nonconformity. After reaching the places of their destination, for a few Sabbaths they will go about and visit the Independent, the Baptist, and the Wesleyan chapels; but, finding neither chapels, ministers, nor congregations, up to their mark in point of respectability, they make their home at the parish church, where the presence of a few country squires, lawyers, and surgeons, will feed their pride. Would that you supplied us with men of better principles! We want men of a different stamp,—men of decided piety and untiring activity, who will not hesitate to use the influence of their position in society, to raise small and obscure churches into prominence, strength, and efficiency; men who would consider it an honour rather than a degradation to attend a prayer-meeting with a handful of working men, or to teach a class of poor children at a Sabbath-school; men who will stand to their principles as Nonconformists with the firmness of martyrs. Send us a few scores of such men, and then you shall not be annoyed any more with applications for money from us.

We look chiefly to the laymen for pecuniary help, but we

N

look to you, ministers, for the spiritual help which we greatly
need, and which you could render us with advantage to yourselves as well as to us. Fifty and sixty years ago, when
three-fourths of the Welsh people were lying in ignorance and
irreligion, David Davies, of Swansea; Christmas Evans; John
Elias; William Williams, of Wern; Ebenezer Morris, and
other ministers of national fame, were accustomed to make
frequent preaching excursions through the length and breadth
of the Principality. These visits of the great preachers
aroused the whole country. The spirits of the ministers were
fired, the churches were revived, and multitudes who never
attended a place of worship were attracted by the fame of the
preachers to go and hear them, and were so affected that they
afterwards became regular hearers and church members. The
universal prevalence of Dissent in Wales is principally to be
ascribed, under God, to the repeated excitements and the
religious interest awakened by the itinerant preaching of our
great preachers.

Why should not a plan which has worked so well with the
Welsh in Wales, be not tried again with the English there?
English brethren, we urgently and affectionately ask you to
make the experiment. If ten or twelve of the very best
preachers among you, were to come down to Wales every
Summer, and go two and two through different districts,
preaching twice a day for a month or five weeks, you would
create a most salutary stirring up of religious emotion among
the English population, and the day of judgment only would
reveal what amount of good you might be the means of doing.
Such work would be a very agreeable exercise for you, during
your holidays. We Welsh ministers do it every year, with
great advantage to both our bodily and mental health. Your
visits would cheer the hearts of the ministers of our infant
English churches, would greatly encourage those Welshmen
who, amidst many discouragements, labour to promote English
preaching; and might possibly be the means of restoring some
of those Englishmen in Wales, who have deserted the ranks
of Nonconformity. We commend these suggestions, dear
brethren, to your prayerful consideration.

You sharp-sighted and enterprising Saxons, have found out
that our barren mountains contain exhaustless treasures of
slate, coal, iron, lead, copper, silver, and gold, and in your
preparations to get at them, you are throwing our hitherto
quiet Wales into a state of commotion, transition, and even

social and religious revolution. We do not begrudge you the hidden treasures of our soil. Take away and welcome, every slate, every lump of coal, every pound of iron, lead, and copper, every ounce of silver, and every grain of gold, which our rocks contain, and while they are being worked out, we will endeavour to get our fair share of the rich spoil; but we conjure you not to take away our free religious institutions, by the introduction of your language and customs into our community, but rather to help us to rescue them from destruction in the transition through which the country begins to pass. If the day is to come—may it be very distant, when the Welsh language shall be no more spoken in the valleys and on the hills of Wales! May that dark day never be seen when evangelical Nonconformity shall cease to be the religion of the majority of its people!

However repugnant to our feelings as Welshmen, would be the annihilation of our language and national customs, and however painful to us all, both Welsh and English, the probability that our Congregationalism shall be weakened, if not destroyed, in the present commotion of society, yet the suposition that a country more thoroughly brought under the influence of evangelical religion than any other country under the sun, may, in passing through a critical change, be converted into a very nest of corruption and irreligion, is incalculably more unbearable. Far be it from us to imagine that Englishmen, Scotchmen, and Irishmen are naturally worse than Welshmen. We are all of us the children of Adam, and too closely bear his corrupt image; but it is a well-known fact that only those districts of the Principality where large numbers of the natives of England and Ireland reside, are notorious for crime and immorality. That fact is easily accounted for. When numbers of people from different parts meet in a country whose language they do not understand, separated from their friends and acquaintances, and the salutary restraints of home, and without any strong religious influence to bear upon them, what can be expected but that they should become corrupt, and the corrupters of all who associate with them? In the year 1860, when the natives of England and Ireland then residing in Wales, could not have been above one-eighth of the population, according to the criminal statistics for that year, they made up 1,651 of our criminals, or nearly one half of the whole number committed throughout the twelve counties.

The following facts may serve to illustrate the striking

difference in point of morality between the Anglicised and the purely Welsh districts of Wales. At Cardiff, where the English element pervades nearly the whole of the people, no less than 2,402 were taken up by the police for various offences during the year ending September, 1865, or nearly one out of every sixteen of the entire population. The number of prostitutes there amounts to 538, and, of course, thieves and drunkards are correspondingly numerous. A sad state of things for a town of little more than forty thousand inhabitants. The morality of Swansea is scarcely, if any better. Bangor, a seaport town in North Wales, supplies us with a happy contrast to this dark picture. Notoriously wicked characters are almost unknown there, and the bulk of the people are more or less under the influence of religion. A few weeks ago the Calvinistic Methodists held their great association in that city, when field-preaching was carried on for two whole days. Finding that most of the business of the town and the work at the neighbouring slate quarries, were to be suspended during the days of the association, a company of strolling players engaged a field to set up a circus, expecting that they would be able to compete with the preachers and get a good share of the people. The religious friends, not being without their fears that that would have been the case, offered them £25 for going away the day before the association, but the offer was rejected with scorn. The following morning the preachers in one field and the players in the other began to proceed with their different employments; but, to the lasting credit of the people of Bangor and the neighbourhood, they all attended the association, leaving the circus men with only a handful of ragged children gazing at their antics. The discouraged players left early the day after, in search of a place where they might be better encouraged. What was done at Bangor would have been done in any other Welsh district of the Principality.

Now, dear brethren, what is to become of Wales? Shall its most religiously pervaded districts be reduced to the morally degraded state of Cardiff, Newport, and Swansea, and similar places? or are we prepared at once, with our combined efforts and earnest prayers, to stand between the dead and the living and try to stay the plague? May the Lord baptize all his ministers and churches throughout Wales and England with a double portion of the spirit of Whitfield, Wesley, Howell Harries, Daniel Rowlands, David Davies, Christmas

Evans, John Elias, and William Williams,—men⁻who were enabled to take the strongholds of Satan by storm, and to pray and preach down the sinful customs of their times! Were we filled with the spirit that moved these men, we could triumphantly lead Wales through her present serious crisis with all her religious institutions not only uninjured, but decidedly improved.

THE GREAT REVIVAL IN SOUTH WALES IN 1849.

TO THE EDITOR OF THE CHRISTIAN WITNESS.

SIR,—In your remarks on the general dearth of revivals of religion in the United Kingdom, on the wrapper of the WIT-NESS for this month, you intimate that no such thing as a revival has been heard of even in Wales during the last twelve years. It affords me the highest gratification to be now able to inform you that powerful awakenings were felt in North Wales in the years 1839 and 1840, and in South Wales in 1841, 1842, and 1843. The circulation of a translation of Mr. Finney's "Lectures," by Mr. Griffiths, of Swansea, was eminently instrumental, in the hand of God, in promoting that ever-memorable revival. The intervening period from the end of the year 1843 to the summer of last year was a season of almost universal spiritual declension; but last year most of the churches in the counties of Monmouth and Glamorgan, and many in those of Brecon and Carmarthen, were blessed with a most powerful revival.

Some months ago, on the suggestion of my excellent friend, Mr. Joseph Maybery, of Llanelly, I wrote to the ministers of those churches which were most signally blessed with these awakenings, for the numbers added to their churches during the year, intimating my intention of publishing the account in one of the periodicals. The following is a list of as many of the churches as furnished me with the numbers added to them. If you will insert it in the CHRISTIAN WITNESS, it will undoubtedly be pondered over with gratification by thousands of your pious readers, and will also be transmitted to future generations as a memorial of the gracious dealings of God with our highly-privileged nation :—

Churches.		Numbers added in 1849.	Ministers.
Brynmawr	...	409	W. Jenkins.
Berea, ditto	...	300	Vacant.
Beaufort	...	396	T. Rees.
Saron, Ebbw Vale	...	180	T. Jeffreys.
Sirhowy	...	280	N. Stephens.
Saron, Tredegar	...	250	D. Evans.
Adullam, ditto	...	50	W. Williams.
Moriah, Rhymney	...	170	E. C. Jenkins.
Zion, ditto	...	130	Vacant.
Zoar, ditto	...	100	J. Thomas,
Goshen, ditto	...	128	Vacant.
Varteg	...	200	M. Jones.
Ebenezer, Pontypool	...	60	E. Rowlands.
Blaenavon	...	96	T. Griffiths.
Nebo, Hirwaun	...	205	W. Williams,
Tabernacle, do. & Salem, Aberdare	...	68	J. Harrison.
Ebenezer, Aberdare	...	146	W. Edwards.
Siloah, ditto	...	124	D. Price.
Cwmbach, ditto	...	38	Vacant.
Aberamman, ditto	...	120	J. Thomas,
Glynnedd	...	90	John Thomas,
Cwmllynfell	...	200	R. Pryse.
Gibeah	...	110	Ditto.
Rhydyfro	...	70	Ditto.
Ystrad-gunlais	...	150	H. Rees.
Godreyribs	...	50	Ditto.
Carmel, Llangiwc	...	128	J. Rees.
Capel Sion, Glais	...	66	Ditto.
Hebron, Clydach	...	109	T. Thomas,
Glandwr	...	156	Ditto.
Libanus, Morriston	...	185	Vacant.

Churches.		Numbers added in 1849.	Ministers.
Horeb, Morriston	...	163	T. Davies.
Alltwen and Pantteg	...	400	P. Griffiths.
Ebenezer, Swansea	...	87	E. Jacob.
Zion Chapel, ditto	...	150	T. Davies.
Zoar, ditto	...	115	R. Rees.
Canaan Chapel, ditto	...	60	E. Watkins.
Bethel, Llansamlet	...	72	Ditto.
Pentre Estyll	...	170	{ T. Davies, Swansea.
Mynyddbach	...	85	J. Davies.
Neath, the two Chapels, about	...	460	{ D. Davies, J. Matthews.
Briton Ferry and Skiwen	...	150	Vacant.
Aberavon	...		{ D. Evans, Neath.
Cwmavon	...	650	{ E. Roberts.
Rock Chapel	...		{ W. Thomas,
Carmel, Maesteg	...	185	W. Morgan.
Zoar, ditto	...	187	Vacant.
Siloh, ditto	...	130	
Cefncribwr and Elim	...	100	Vacant.
Bridgend and Coity	...	60	J. D. Williams.
Llanelly, Breconshire	...	160	J. Davies.
Llangynidr	...	62	S. Phillips.
Bwlchnewydd	...	170	Vacant.
Capel Sion	...	50	J. Evans,
Pontyberem	...	120	Ditto.
Pembrey	...	115	H. Evans.
Nazareth	...	130	D. Evans.
Bethania, Llannon	...	100	H. Davies.
Llannybree	...	120	W. James.
Cross Inn	...	125	R. Powell.

The foregoing list is, of course, imperfect, as it scarcely contains one-half of the churches which were blessed by the wonderful revival of last year. It is supposed that from 1,200 to 1,500 persons were added to the nine Congregational churches in the parish of Merthyr Tydvil, and at least 1,000 to the churches in Carmarthenshire besides those in the above list, such as Llandovery, Llangadock, Llandilo, Carmarthen, Llanelly, &c.   •

One very peculiar feature of this wonderful movement was, the great numbers of converts who pressed together, at the same time, to the anxious meetings. In some localities meetings for conversing with the awakened were held every evening throughout the week, and sometimes oftener; and from twenty to thirty individuals were examined at each meeting. Mr. Hughes, of Dowlais, gave the right hand of fellowship to *two hundred and forty* persons the same Sabbath morning, on their admission to the Lord's Supper; and ·your correspondent had the soul-cheering gratification of doing the same to *two hundred and ten* on the 28th of October last.

These gracious visitations of the Spirit of God were not confined to the Congregational churches. Some thousands were added to the Baptist churches in the counties of Monmouth and Glamorgan, and great numbers joined the Calvinistic and Wesleyan Methodist Societies in some localities.

Many good warm-hearted old Christians had their doubts of the reality of these movements, because they were not attended by loud cries, promiscuous singing, jumping, &c., as some former revivals were; but the audible groans of hundreds, and the floods of tears shed under the preaching of the word, clearly manifested some strong inward feelings, which the eloquence or the schemes of man could not effect; and what is still a more convincing proof that it was a work of the Spirit of God, the thousands of young converts, with comparatively rare exceptions, are walking worthy of their holy profession.

It will be readily acknowledged that the terrible visitation of the *Cholera* was principally the means of arousing the attention of our hearers to consider seriously the important truths with which they were already theoretically acquainted; but who will venture to deny that the Lord had mercifully ordained this awful scourge as the means of accomplishing his gracious purpose of saving thousands?

The mighty movements are not felt now as they were eight

or nine months ago in any place; but things wear a very encouraging aspect. Almost all the churches are peaceful; the attendance on the means of grace is unparalleled in the history of religion amongst us; our youth manifest great thirst for religious knowledge; our Sabbath-schools are very flourishing; a number of pious and talented young men are preparing for the ministry; and many of the young ministers who were ordained within the last six years are very active and promising.

The Welsh is now one of the most religious nations on the face of the earth. Nine-tenths of the middle and working classes are either professors of religion or constant attendants on the means of grace. Evangelical religion in Wales has the public opinion decidedly in its favour. But, alas! we are, as a nation, after all, very far from what we ought to be. Sin and Satan are still amongst us, and the time is not yet come for the people of God to take their rest. May the Spirit of the Lord continue to pour his blessings upon us, and may his mighty power be felt amongst the millions of England, and throughout the whole wide world!

I am, Dear Sir,

Yours in the bonds of the Gospel,

THOMAS REES.

Beaufort, near Abergavenny,
May 7, 1850.

––––––––––

THE IRISH AND WELSH REVIVALS IN 1859.

The following letters were addressed to Mr. H. O. Wills, of Bristol, who, with his brother, Mr. W. D. Wills, Mr. S. Morley, Mr. C. Jupe, and Mr. I. Perry, generously offered at the Congregational Union Meetings at Aberdare, to supply the writer, with four other Welsh Ministers, with the means of visiting the scenes of the Irish Revivals.

Beaufort, Oct. 19, 1859.

Dear Sir,—Having through your kindness been enabled to visit the scenes of the Religious Revivals in Ireland, I avail myself of the first opportunity after my return to furnish you with some account of my visit.

On Tuesday morning, the 4th inst., in company with my beloved brethren, the Revs. John Davies, of Aberaman, David Price and John Cunnick, of Aberdare; William Williams, of Hirwain; and Noah Stephens and Mr. John Evans, of Liverpool, I started for Ireland. On our arrival at Holyhead that evening, we found that we had been announced to preach there. After travelling more than 200 miles, of course we felt fatigued; but as four crowded congregations in the Independent, the Calvinistic Methodist, the Wesleyan, and the Baptist chapels were anxiously waiting for us, we had to proceed at once from the railway carriage to the pulpits, and notwithstanding the disadvantages under which we laboured, the services proved exceedingly comfortable and soul-refreshing to ourselves and our hearers. Having rested a few hours at a friend's house, we took our berths in the saloon of the mail steamer for Dublin. Those of us who could, slept; and between six and seven on Wednesday morning we landed at Kingstown. At one o'clock we left Dublin for Belfast. The first religious service which we attended there was a prayer-meeting at the vestry of the Rev. R. Knox's church. This meeting is held daily for half-an-hour, for the benefit of the factory girls. These girls have only three-quarters of an hour allowed them for dinner-time, and of this they devote half-an-hour for the prayer-meeting, having only the remaining fifteen minutes to dine. Their dinner consists of a few biscuits or bread and butter, which they eat on their way back from the meeting to the factory. We attended this interesting meeting twice during our short stay at Belfast, and found there each time from sixty to seventy girls, who all appeared very intelligent, attentive, and devotional. One of us was present at a prayer-meeting which is held daily in a sawpit on Queen's Island, near Belfast, by the ship-carpenters working there. The time allotted for this meeting also is only half-an-hour. The attendance was about seventy, and the short prayers and addresses of the working men were most appropriate and earnest. We noticed and felt at all the prayer-meetings which we were able to attend, evident proofs of a revived religious feeling. One of the elders of the Rev. Thomas Toye's church told me that that church, previous to the revival, held a prayer-meeting every evening for a whole year, and that during the present awakening above 800 souls were convinced, if not converted, in their place of worship. Is not this fact worthy of the prayerful consideration of every minister and church throughout Christendom? We made it a point to visit every part of the town early in the morning, at all hours during the day, and even late in the evening, and to gather all the information we could from ministers, town missionaries, shopkeepers, policemen, cabmen, etc., respecting the 'Revival,' and all bore testimony in its favour, with only one exception. That person, I presume, was a Roman Catholic. He told us that 'this revivalism' had very much injured trade, and made people conceited and cool towards their neighbours. He probably meant the trades of the publicans, the publishers of irreligious books, and the Roman Catholic priests. It is certain that the revival has not injured any good trade. A bookseller, who employs a great number of travelling agents, told us that previous to the revival movement, he used to sell weekly, in the province of Ulster, above 120,000 copies of novels, non-religious periodicals, etc., but that the sale of such literary trash is now reduced to less than one-third, while the demand for religious books has increased proportionably. During our stay at Belfast, we did not hear an oath, nor see a drunkard. The population of that town amounts to 120,000. Is there a town of one-fourth that population in England or Wales, where seven observing strangers in four days would not have met with many drunkards, and heard many profane oaths?

On Friday afternoon we left Belfast for Armagh. Having previously corresponded with the Rev. R. H. Craig, the Independent minister there, we were announced to address a meeting that evening on the revivals in Wales. Our Irish brethren were as anxious to know what God is doing in Wales as we were to know what he is doing amongst them. Soon after seven o'clock the Independent Chapel, which will seat from 500 to 600, was well filled by a respectable and most attentive congregation. Finding that it was ten o'clock when only three of us had spoken, the congregation expressed an earnest desire to have a second meeting on Saturday evening. That was again well attended, and we have grounds to hope that the good tidings which we were able to communicate will strengthen the hands and cheer the hearts of our revived brethren at Armagh. On Sabbath morning one of the brethren went to Doneghmore, another to Moy, and a third to Richhill, where they preached to crowded congregations. I preached at Armagh, to one of the most attentive and melting congregations I ever saw. In the evening I preached for the

Rev. W. Bagley, at Belfast. How pleasant and easy it is to address people prepared by the Spirit of God to receive the word with joy! My friends, Davies and Stephens, were preaching on Sunday afternoon in a large barn, a few miles out of Armagh, to a very numerous audience, and during the service a young man was 'prostrated.' As soon as he became able to speak, he cried most earnestly for mercy. On Monday evening we attended a most interesting prayer-meeting with Mr. Bagley and his people at Belfast; and this was the last of a series of memorable religious services which we had the privilege of enjoying during our brief sojourn in Ireland. We never spent six days in a more happy and heavenly frame of mind.

After making the most diligent inquiry, the most careful observations, and exercising the most impartial judgment which we were capable of exercising, we arrived at the conclusion, that the Irish Revival is a great reality, and that all the accounts of it, which we read previous to our personal visit, fell far short of giving us an adequate idea of the glorious movement.

With all the pleasing things which we met with in Ireland, we found some to grieve us. 1. The feeble state of our own denomination. Independency is not by any means a religious power in Ireland. If we did not misunderstand the character of the people, Ulster is a fine field for the development of our principles. The Irish people, like the Welsh, are open, sociable, lively, and passionately fond of liberty. Itinerant preaching has done more than anything else to raise Congregationalism in Wales, and we are firmly persuaded that the same thing would be a life from the dead to Congregationalism in Ireland. If twenty or thirty of our most popular English ministers were to devote a month or six weeks every year, to preach once or twice a-day in the towns, the villages, the rural districts of Ireland, they would find it a most healthy exercise, and most blessed results would undoubtedly follow. Our Irish brethren would most gladly receive and assist them, and their drooping hearts would be cheered by such visits. And why should not the two societies which we have for the evangelisation of Ireland be amalgamated, and their income at once trebled? The two excellent brethren of our denomination in Ireland, with whom we had the happiness of conversing, Mr. Bagley, of Belfast, and Mr. Craig, of Armagh, were not a little cheered by our visit to them: how much more would their

hearts be gladdened, and the principles which they represent
be popularised, if their pulpits were occupied five or six times
every year by the leading men of our denomination in England.
When our popular preachers wish to exchange the smoky
atmosphere of the large English towns for a purer air, let them
go over to Ireland for a month or two, preaching twice a-day,
and travelling twenty or thirty Irish miles, and I am certain
that they would return to their homes with braced nerves and
renewed strength, and the day of judgment alone would reveal
how much good they would do.

2. We were also grieved by finding that the Protestants
of the sister island are divided and sub-divided into a great
number of sects. The Presbyterians are split into no less
than six different bodies, and the Methodists, as they are in
England, into three or four. What valid reason can be assign-
ed for this needless waste of power? While agreeing in
doctrine and the leading principles of ecclesiastical polity, do
they stand guiltless before the Great Head of the Church by
standing aloof from one another? If the five smaller Presbyterian bodies conscientiously object to the unhappy connection
of the Irish Presbyterian Church with the State, why should
not they be amalgamated into one body? The Church of
Rome, the curse of Ireland, does not divide and weaken her
strength for evil; and why should the Protestants, by their
frivolous divisions, enfeeble their influence for good? Let us
hope and pray that this blessed revival, while increasing the
number of pious Protestants, may also lessen the number of
sects.

On our way to Ireland, the friends at Holyhead would not
leave us until we made them a promise to hold there a revival
meeting on our return, and Wednesday, the 12th inst., was
fixed upon as the day to hold it. When we arrived there on
Tuesday evening, the 11th, we were informed that the *Great
Eastern* was there a day before us, and that on Wednesday
excursion trains and steamers would pour thousands of visitors
from the North of England and North Wales into the town.
For this reason it was generally feared that the revival meeting would prove a failure, and that it was a mistake to announce it to be held on such a day. But all our fears were removed when we found the spacious chapel more than half full
between nine and ten o'clock in the morning. Two of us
preached at that service, and a most heavenly feeling pervaded
the whole congregation. In the afternoon almost every sitting

was occupied, and in the evening the place was crammed. At the afternoon and the evening services the effect was quite overpowering. Floods of tears were shed, and the vast multitude at times burst out into loud sobbing. I do not expect to witness a more glorious sight till I get to heaven. We were, like the priests in the Temple, not able to stand to minister by reason of the cloud of glory which filled the place. It is hoped that this is the commencement of a great revival which will spread through the whole island of Anglesea. The churches in Caernarvonshire have been blessed with a powerful revival for some time. There is scarcely a church of any denomination in the northern part of that county which has not had added to it from twenty to two hundred members within the last three months.

On Thursday, the 13th, we addressed two large meetings of Welsh people at Liverpool on the subject of religious revivals. These also were meetings which are not soon, if ever, to be forgotten.

Last Friday we reached our homes in safety, and found our families and churches happy and comfortable. During this short tour we have received much good, and we trust that we have also been the means of doing some good. We bless the Lord for putting it in your heart, and in the hearts of your friends, to send us out, like Barnabas, to see the grace of God.

I am, dear Sir,

Yours in the Gospel of Christ,

THOMAS REES.

H. O. Wills, Esq., Bristol.

Beaufort, November 11, 1859.

Dear Sir,—I am happy to be able to inform you that the revival is progressing continually in Wales. This neighbourhood is not the scene of those powerful movements which are felt in many other districts, but a few are added to my church almost every week, and the other churches throughout the district are similarly blessed. Last month fifty-five members of my church and eighty-five of the Rev. T. Jeffreys' church (of Ebbw Vale) were dismissed to form a new interest in a populous locality between Beaufort and Ebbw Vale, and on the 30th ult. Mr. Jeffreys and myself administered the ordinance of the Lord's Supper to the newly-formed church. We have not the least doubt but that the places of our beloved friends who left us shall soon be filled by additions from the world, and the earnest prayers of the mother churches is that the infant cause may soon grow into a strong and powerful one.

The Vale of Glamorgan, as far as richness of soil and beauty of scenery are concerned, is the garden of South Wales, but until now true religion had made but very little progress there. While the hilly and most barren parts of the country had their large chapels and flourishing congregations, the chapels in the rich vale were small, shabby in appearance, and with few exceptions badly attended. However, this year the arm of the Lord is made bare even there. Hundreds have been converted in the district between Cardiff and Bridgend within the last few months. Many robust men and hardened sinners are melted down, and weep like children under the preaching of the Gospel and at the prayer-meetings. May the God who has adorned the Vale of Glamorgan with natural beauty, by the influence of his Spirit adorn it also with moral beauty.

The parish of Festiniog, one of the most hilly districts of the mountainous county of Merioneth, has lately been blessed with a most powerful awakening. The population of this place is from five to six thousand. Most of the people are employed in the slate quarries, the property of Lord Palmerston and others. Here the Calvinistic Methodists have four congregations, the Independents three, the Episcopalians two, and the Wesleyans one. Each of these congregations have had their respective shares of the fruits of the present revival. From five to six hundred persons have been hopefully converted in this parish since the beginning of last month, and amongst the converts there are some of the most careless and daring sinners in the place.

The following instances of remarkable conversions will not be uninteresting to you. Two men were lately returning home from a beershop at a very late hour, and one of them said to the other, "When I get into the house to-night my wife will scold me dreadfully." "Oh," said his companion, "I shall have something ten times more intolerable than scolding: my wife is always quiet, but she weeps and speaks to me about my soul, and her words are burning like fire in my conscience."

Having reached his house, his wife, as he expected, met him at the door weeping. He retired to his bed immediately and slept, but his pious wife could not sleep. She wrestled with her God for hours on his behalf. About three o'clock in the morning he awoke and saw her standing at the bedside and wetting his face and pillow with her warm tears. "Margaret," said he, "what is the matter with you?" She replied, "the thought that my dear husband is an enemy to my beloved Saviour, and that he is likely to have his eternal portion with damned spirits, almost breaks my heart." This was too much for him, he rose and knelt by his wife and prayed for mercy. They are now a happy couple rejoicing in the hope of dwelling together for ever in heaven.

At a village in North Wales there was a young man, who though young, had become so hardened as to laugh at the tears and prayers of his pious mother. One evening in the first week of last month, he stood outside the windows of the village chapel, to mock the good people who were holding a prayer-meeting there. An elderly woman seeing him mildly rebuked him, but his insolent reply was, "Go you and serve your Master, and let me alone to serve mine." A few minutes after he was found lying in the road with his face to the ground. A person happening to pass raised him up, and having recognised him, inquired what ailed him, "I do not know," said he, "unless God is about to kill me; I am very ill." His sickness, however, was not unto death, but for the glory of God. He was taken home and laid on the bed. For some days he suffered the most dreadful mental agony, but at length found peace in believing, and this mocker is now one of the most earnest men of prayer in the village. As the arm of the Lord is strong enough to pluck such brands from the burning, let us continue earnest in prayer for the conversion of such characters.

With these cheering facts I must close for the present, but I hope to be able to furnish you with a further account of God's wonders in the Principality at a future time.

I am, dear Sir,

Yours with Christian affection,

THOMAS REES.

H. O. Wills, Esq., Bristol.

Beaufort, December 24, 1859.
Sir,—Since the date of my last letter to you the Lord has done wonders amongst us. The Revival continues to gain ground in almost every part of the Principality. The Welsh newspapers are filled every week with cheering reports of the progress and the blessed effects of the mighty movement throughout South and North Wales. The Revival is the principal subject of conversation in the markets and fairs, and scarcely a letter passes through the post which does not contain something concerning it. In most localities this is the all-absorbing subject.

It is a fact worthy to be recorded, that the students in our Colleges at Bala and Brecon, are in a most remarkable measure baptised with a Revival spirit. When the Bala students returned to College after their summer vacation, several of them arrived warm from the scenes of the most powerful awakenings, and these communicated their earnest spirit to their less revived fellow students. By degrees the church was affected; professors were aroused from their slumbers; prayer-meetings were multiplied, and the whole town is now moved. One of the students in a letter to me on the 8th instant says, that above forty were then added to the Congregational Church at Bala; that they hold prayer-meetings twice every day, and that the ardency of their feelings is such that they seldom sleep till three or four o'clock in the morning. These young men are going out every Sabbath to supply the congregations in the surrounding country, and the hand of the Lord is with them wherever they go.

The Calvinistic Methodists have also a College at Bala, and their students like ours, are "full of the Holy Spirit and of faith." The young men of the two Institutions often meet for social prayer and religious conversation; and they even go to many prayerless families in the town to conduct family worship.

Many of the students in the Independent College at Brecon are also full of the Revival fire, and their Sabbath visits to the neighbouring churches are eminently blessed. Seven of them are gone this week to North Wales, not to spend their Christmas holidays in idleness, but to preach and conduct Revival meetings every day. This excitement may, to some extent, retard the progress of the young men with their studies; but the churches will not regret their deficiency in human learning, however useful it may be, when they find that they are made wise to win souls.

The limits of this letter will not allow me to name all the places which are blessed with the Revival, much less to furnish you with a minute account of it in every locality; I shall, therefore, only refer to a few districts where it has broken out with remarkable power within the last six weeks.

Ever since the memorable meeting which we had at Holyhead, on our return from Ireland, the work of the Lord is progressing in that town, and several hundreds have been added to the churches. It has also spread throughout Anglesea. The town of Denbigh has for the last four or five weeks been the scene of a most wonderful work of grace. Union prayer-meetings are held once or twice every week, in which all the Dissenting denominations unite. From November 27th to December 5th nearly two hundred were added to the different churches, in the following proportions:—To the Calvinistic Methodists, 78; to the Independents, 60; to the Wesleyans, 40; and to the Baptists, 10.

Some of the students from Bala have been instrumental in originating a powerful movement at Corwen, Cynwyd, and Llandrillo, in Merionethshire, since the beginning of this month. The town of Dolgelly, in the same county, and the country around it are abundantly blessed. A most heavenly feeling pervades the Welsh churches at Liverpool and Birkenhead, and many are constantly added to them. The county of Caernarvon is as lively as ever. In a word, almost every church throughout North Wales is more or less moved.

In South Wales, where the work originated about twelve months ago, it progresses most favourably, though, perhaps, not so universally as in the North. Many churches in Breconshire are now experiencing the powers of the world to come to a greater degree than they ever did, at least, in the present age. The ancient Congregational Church at Llangattock, Crickhowell, after a long and dreary winter, is now beginning to enjoy times of refreshing from the presence of the Lord. Several small congregations in the neighbourhood of Builth have had their numbers doubled within the last few weeks.

Cwmcamlais is a small secluded place between the mountains, about six miles out of Brecon. The adult population of the valley does not exceed 150. The Congregational Church, which is the only religious society in the district, consisted of

P

forty members. Some of these are very old, and have adorned
their profession of religion for above sixty years. These aged
Christians have for a long time been longing and praying for
a gracious visit from the Lord before their departure, and on
the 11th instant their prayers were answered. A most powerful and irresistible influence was felt by the whole congregation. Since that day from twenty to thirty joined the
church, and the earnest expectation and prayers of all the
friends of religion there are, that the Lord may continue to
pour down his Spirit until every soul in the valley is brought
to the Saviour. Mr. Stephens, the minister, in a letter to me
this week, expresses himself thus :—" The Lord has graciously
visited the small church at Cwmcamlais. The old members
are quite overcome with joy, and the hearers flock into the
church. About twenty have joined it this week. Do come
to see us, and give us two or three sermons. It does
not matter what day you come—the Sabbath or a week-day—
for every day is a Sabbath with us now. The people cannot
think of doing anything but feed their cattle, and attend the
prayer-meetings. In your last letter you remind me that we
are growing old. All the better, my dear brother, for we are
drawing nearer to heaven."

The Congregational, and the Calvinistic Methodist Churches
at Ebbw-vale in this county, are blessed with a large measure
of Divine influence. At a prayer-meeting in the Independent
Chapel (Mr. Jeffreys') on Monday evening, the 12th inst., the
attendance being unusually large, a person, who had been a
member of the church for nearly twenty years, was requested
to engage in prayer. Having uttered a few sentences, he
began to pray for the conversion of his aged father in the
most pathetic expressions. His feelings soon overpowered
him, and in an instant the whole congregation were so
affected that they burst out into loud sobbing. When the
intensity of the feeling had somewhat subsided, the Minister
requested those of the hearers who had a desire to join the
church, to remain behind. Thirteen did so, and amongst
others the father of this man. The grey-headed sinner came
weeping to the communion table to be spoken to.

Scarcely any physical prostrations occur, but the intensity
of feeling manifested is often remarkable. Last Sabbath evening, at Libanus Chapel, near Brecon, those of the congregation
who were affected were invited to stay after the close of the
public service with the members. At a later hour the chapel-

keeper, while locking the doors, overheard a person groaning in the adjoining graveyard. He went in, and to his surprise found a young man there in the greatest mental agony. It appears that he was too timid to remain with the candidates in the chapel, and too much affected to go home.

Some time ago, in the neighbourhood of Swansea, a dissolute young man, the eldest son of a widow, was one Sabbath evening on the roadside waiting for his wicked companions. A religious man passing on his way to chapel, invited him to accompany him to the house of God. He reluctantly consented to go, and it was well for him that he did so. The Spirit of God that evening touched his heart. His mother, who was not in chapel, wondered to see him returning home so early. A few minutes after a younger brother came in and told his mother,—" We had a very strange meeting to-night. Every one was weeping there, and my brother Daniel wept also." It is easier to imagine than to describe what were the feelings of the mother at this unexpected change in her wild and undutiful son. That young man, ever since that memorable Sabbath evening, has led a new life.

I am, dear Sir,

Yours with Christian affection,

THOMAS REES.

H. O. Wills, Esq., Bristol.

The churches of Wales have had no *revival* in the usual acceptation of that term since the years 1859—60. Several thousands were added to the Nonconformist churches of the Counties of Monmouth, Glamorgan, and Carmarthen, last year (1866), but no excitement and deep religious feeling, the usual attendants on revivals in former years, were experienced in any congregation. Still it is to be hoped that many sincere and earnest persons have joined our religious societies who will walk worthy of their profession, and prove eminently useful in their different spheres.

SWANSEA:
PRINTED BY E. GRIFFITHS, HIGH-STREET.

www.ingramcontent.com/pod-product-compliance
Lightning Source LLC
Chambersburg PA
CBHW032103010726
47493CB00008B/2509